IRELAND IN WORLD COMMERCE

Ireland in World Commerce

BY

CHARLES HULTMAN

UNIVERSITY OF KENTUCKY,
LEXINGTON, KENTUCKY

THE MERCIER PRESS
4 BRIDGE STREET, CORK

First published in the Netherlands
Made and printed in Holland by Bosch, Utrecht

PREFACE

This small volume has been written primarily with the interests of economics students in mind. It is designed to supplement other books on international economics and trade as well as those books concerned largely with the Irish economy. This book hopefully gains its special character as an analysis of the position of the small, open country in the world economy with particular reference to the institutions and features characteristic of Ireland. Thus an extensive treatment is afforded such topics as the balance of payments adjustment process for an open economy, the implications of unrestricted factor movements, and the regional arrangements in which Ireland might participate. Many topics are treated briefly; students desiring an extensive treatment of such subjects as the development of classical trade theory or the instruments of international finance should turn to one of several standard works (some of which are listed in the bibliography).

It is also assumed that as a foundation for further development of international economic analysis, the student must become familiar with some of the techniques and the findings of professional economists. Accordingly, an effort has been made to note the contributions of other writers who have examined problems of an international character.

A number of issues of immediate national importance are examined – Ireland and the European Economic Community, free trade and protection, emigration, and the implications of borrowing from abroad. In each instance, an effort is made to include sufficient information and the analytical tools to provide the basis for an exploration of the economic aspects of each question, rather than offering settled conclusions. Many other factors – political, social and religious – have a bearing on the answers and solutions which are 'right' for the Irish economy; these must be taken into consideration in determining the appropriateness of policy decisions.

For assistance in making this publication possible, the following persons are to be acknowledged: Professor David O'Mahony, for encouragement and for reading an early draft of the manuscript; Mr Donald Nunan, for reading the manuscript; Professor Marina von Neumann Whitman, University of Pittsburgh, for comments on an analytical chapter; Irene E. Hultman, for editorial assistance;

Miss Sheila Brennan, for supplying library material; and Miss Maura Collins, for typing assistance. The author assumes full responsibility for any defects.

Research for the volume was undertaken when the author was Fulbright Lecturer, at University College, Cork.

TABLE OF CONTENTS

INTRODUCTION

A basic difference between commerce among countries and commerce within a country pertains to the existence and implications of political boundaries. In the absence of such man-made arrangements, an analysis of the economics of specialization and exchange would be largely the same in either case. But the development of states and political boundaries has promulgated a set of attitudes, policies and institutional arrangements which has made it convenient to study international economics as a separate part of economic analysis.

Nations create their own monetary facilities, legal framework, tax systems and other institutions for accommodating economic activity; attitudes develop which are essentially nationalistic in nature. Internal objectives relating to prices, employment and economic growth take precedence over external matters. Tariffs, quotas and protective devices are used in varying degrees of restrictiveness in the hope that they will facilitate the achievement of internal goals. As a result, commodities, capital and people move less freely across national boundaries than within a country. Commerce between countries is also subject to an additional risk because of the possibility of abrupt and arbitrary change in commercial policy on the part of importing nations. External, as well as internal, commerce is generally conducted by private persons and firms but foreign trade is more likely to be affected by nationalistic policies on the part of governments.

Certain other differences are more physical in nature. Generally, although not always, international trade involves greater distances and higher transportation costs. Geographical distances also contribute to an unfamiliarity with laws, language, customs and consumer tastes of other lands and thus inhibit the flow of trade. The development of modern communication and transportation has alleviated the magnitude of such differences but has not necessarily similarly affected the significance of national sovereignty.

National entities not only encompass but also contribute to a unique set of attitudes and demand conditions, resources and supply conditions. As a result, a country represents an area with a relative resource endowment (land, labour, capital and entrepreneurial ability) unlike that existing anywhere else. Further, the differential endowment of resources among areas (or nations) is considered to be the most important factor causing differences in costs between areas (or nations) and thus providing the basis for trade or an exchange of goods and services. At the same time, however, the line of causation may run in the other direction; trade may be both a cause as well as a result of such inequality.

Unequal factor endowments are the result of accidents of geography with respect to climate and natural resources, and social attitudes with respect to a wide range of factors–savings, profit-seeking, family size, education, etc. The extent to which one nation differs from others also depends upon its relative size and degree of openness. These two factors, *size and openness*, greatly affect the nature of the relationship between a nation's domestic productive structure and its external economic activity, and between its domestic goals and its commercial policy with respect to the rest of the world.

The manner in which the small, open economy pursues internal economic objectives and external commercial policies is greatly influenced by exogenous economic and political forces. Unlike a large and closed economy, the small country has less freedom to pursue independent monetary and fiscal policies consistent with national economic objectives. Generally, the small country, if it is to remain 'open' and thus use its resources in an efficient fashion, must adjust or modify its economic policies in accordance with those established by the large trading nations.

The Republic of Ireland, with a population of 2.9 million, a gross national product of £ 1,146 million, and a foreign trade ratio of almost 80 per cent is an example of such an economy. If Ireland is to remain active in, and secure the benefits of, world commerce, she is somewhat restricted in the use of fiscal policy (e.g., deficit government spending) to promote full employment, lest her balance of payments position deteriorate. For the same reason she must watch more closely the relationship between productivity gains and increases in the wage rate. Finally, an 'acceptable' degree of inflation in Ireland is determined largely by price developments in the United Kingdom, Europe, the United States, and other trading partners. No country, of course, has complete freedom to pursue independent domestic policies if it is to retain its position in world trade and investment; yet it remains true that the degree of freedom is closely related to the size and openness of the economy.

'Small' and 'open' as concepts. Typically, the small economy is also an open one. This, however, is not an accident of geography, politics, or nature; economic considerations dictate that this be the case. That is, in the interests of efficiency in the use of resources,

the small country finds it essential to participate actively in world trade. Numerous countries might be cited as illustrations. Among the industrialized countries, in addition to Ireland, it would include Austria, Belgium, Denmark, the Netherlands, Sweden and Switzerland; it also includes many of the less developed nations located in Africa and South America.

As is true in most instances, it is easier to identify than to define a concept; there is no satisfactory way to define 'small' and 'open' in order that they are useful for all analytical purposes. Initially, though, it is to be realized that the two concepts are relative in nature and have no meaning in an absolute sense. That is, a country is 'small' or 'open' only in comparison with other countries. An open economy might be defined as one in which the foreign trade sector (i.e., industries in which exports or imports play an important role) is large in comparison with all other domestic sectors. Such an economy is also frequently active in world capital or money markets, either as a net borrower or lender. The degree of openness of an economy is sometimes measured in quantitative terms with the foreign trade ratio:

$$\frac{exports + imports}{gross\ national\ product}$$

Ireland is one of the most open economies in the world today and there are indications that the foreign trade sector will become increasingly important. Ireland's openness is even more accentuated by two other considerations; (i) Irish citizens may move freely to and from Britain and (ii) payments for transactions between Britain and Ireland are made by cheque in the same way as payments for transactions within Ireland.

A small economy might be defined as one in which the level of aggregate spending, or output, or economic activity (determined by the size of the population and per capita income) is low relative to that of other countries. Accordingly, Ireland with an annual per capita income of approximately £350 but with an unusually small population must be regarded as a small economy, especially in comparison with other industrialized countries. Further, the potential productive capacity of the economy is diminished somewhat since, because of emigration, a relatively smaller share of the population is in the productive age bracket (ages 15-64).

In addition to the foreign trade orientation and small population, the typical small country is less diversified in its production than the large nation. 'Balanced' growth and development are lacking in the sense that internal production does not closely match the diversity of consumer and producer demands. The small economy's export sector is usually not diversified; in many instances, a significant share of its exports is directed toward a single country. Insofar as a small geographical area is frequently involved, it usually possesses a limited variety of natural resources. The domestic market is also small and by itself may prevent certain firms and industries from securing the full advantage of economies of large scale production. In addition, and because of these various factors, the structural interdependence between various industries and sectors is less than for a large economy.

The Republic of Ireland is about 27 thousand square miles in area; by European standards it is not densely populated. In 1966, almost 55 per cent of the value of her exports took the form of live animals, food and food preparations, and about 70 per cent of total exports were directed toward the United Kingdom.

Irish planning and the external sector. Ireland's willingness, or perhaps determination, to become active in world commerce has been especially pronounced with the establishment of the Organization for European Economic Cooperation in the late 1940's and European efforts at trade liberalization. In an earlier period (the 1930's), Irish commercial policy became restrictive partially as a result of difficulties with Britain and also as a reaction to the world-wide depression and the protectionist policies pursued by other countries.

A policy of trade liberalization and industrial export promotion was reflected in the Government's First Programme for Economic Expansion (1959-1963). The Second Programme, which was instituted in 1964, was more explicit in its objectives. It established a target figure which would lead to a 150 per cent increase in industrial exports from 1960 to 1970. Industry is being provided inducement for expansion through the use of generous direct subsidies, but with the proviso that companies must eventually be competitive with overseas firms. In general, it appears that success of the entire Programme is closely related to the degree of success achieved in the export sector. If this sector performs the role assigned it in the Second Programme, Ireland will become an even more open economy by 1970 in the sense that the foreign trade ratio will become larger.

CHAPTER I

NATURE OF THE IRISH ECONOMY

According to international trade theory, a country exports items which embody a large proportion of its abundant factor of production. Imported items are largely those requiring substantial amounts of the factor of production which are relatively scarce within the economy. But exports and imports, in turn, affect the relative quantity and quality of an economy's resources. It is apparent in examining the Republic of Ireland that the structure of the domestic economy and its external trade are closely inter-related. If Ireland were a more self-sufficient economy, or less dependent on external trade, the output potential of her agricultural sector and industry would be considerably different. The heavy dependence on external trade has lessened the structural inter-dependence of industries within the economy.

Sources and uses of income. A survey of the nature of the economy of Ireland might begin with an examination of the major aggregates of the national income accounts to determine the derivation of total income and production. National income of the Republic can be measured either by sector of origin or by category of income. Ireland's net domestic product or income in 1967 amounted to £867 million (Table I–1). The largest single share of the total (£291 million or 34 per cent) originated in industry; this is also the sector which has evidenced the most rapid growth in recent years. Income originating in agriculture, forestry and fishing accounted for almost 20 per cent of the total; distribution and transport, almost 18 per cent of the total.

In terms of factoral returns or categories of income, agricultural wages, salaries and profits in 1967 represented almost 20 per cent of total national income (Table I–2). The major category was non-agricultural wages, salaries and pensions, which amounted to about 60 per cent of the total.

The figure for gross national product (GNP) – the market value of all final goods and services produced – can be determined from national income by making adjustments for depreciation, external trade, indirect taxes and subsidies. Ireland's GNP, in terms of expenditures for various major categories, is presented in Table I–3 for 1967. Of a GNP of £ 1,146 million, by far the greatest share, almost 70 per cent, is personal expenditure on consumers' goods and services. Gross domestic fixed capital formation, an

TABLE I-1

NET DOMESTIC INCOME BY SECTOR OF ORIGIN, 1967

(in millions of pounds)

Sector	Amount
Agriculture, forestry and fishing	£172
Industry	291
Distribution and transport	153
Public administration and defence	57
Other sectors	194
Total Net Domestic Income	£867

Source: *Review of 1967 and Outlook for 1968*. Dublin: Stationery Office, 1968, p. 36.

important item affecting the growth potential of the economy, amounted to £212 million, or about 19 per cent of GNP; this percentage, which includes both government and private investment, has increased in recent years and yet is relatively low when compared with that of most European countries. Well over one-third of Ireland's gross investment is in various types of agricultural, industrial and transport equipment and machinery; about one-third is in building and construction (excluding dwellings but including land rehabilitation); about one-fourth is in roads and dwellings.

Because GNP reflects goods and services *actually produced* within the economy, commodity imports are not included as one of its components. It will be noted from Table I-3 that the value of imports exceeded the value of exports by about £33 million. The difference is related to the economy's external capital movements for the year; it also indicates that the amount of commodities consumed and used for investment purposes exceeded the amount of production during the year.

Sources of employment. The structure of the Irish economy for 1967 is also reflected in the source of employment of the labour force (Table I-4). Of a total labour force of 1,120,000, almost 29 per cent, or 322 thousand, are employed in agriculture, forestry and fishing – although, as noted earlier, this sector produced only about 20 per cent of national income. Manufacturing industries are second in importance, employing 201 thousand workers, or almost 18 per cent of the total. Manufacturing, along with building and construction, are the only branches of economic activity

TABLE I–2
NET DOMESTIC INCOME BY CATEGORIES
OF INCOME, 1967

(in millions of pounds)

Category	Amount
Agricultural wages and salaries	£ 19
Agricultural profits	150
Non-agricultural wages, salaries and pensions	520
Non-agricultural other income	178
Total Net Domestic Income	£867

Source: *Review of 1967 and Outlook for 1968,* Dublin: Stationery Office, 1968, p. 35.

TABLE I–3
EXPENDITURE ON GROSS NATIONAL
PRODUCT, 1967

(in millions of pounds)

Category	Amount
Personal expenditure on consumers' goods and services	£ 780
Net expenditure by public authorities on current goods and services	144
Gross domestic fixed capital formation	212
Exports of goods and services	388
less Imports of goods and services	421
Net factor income from abroad	43
Gross National Product	£1,146

Source: *Review of 1967 and Outlook for 1968.* Dublin: Stationery Office, 1968, p. 37.

showing any substantial increase in employment in the last several years. During the same period, the number employed in agricultural, forestry and fishing activities has declined sharply. Actually the decline in the rural population over the past 100 years is roughly equal to the fall in total population over the same period, largely as a result of emigration. Employment in remaining branches of activity, most of which might be included in the 'service' sector, has evidenced only a slight gain in recent years.

17

EMPLOYMENT BY MAIN BRANCH OF ACTIVITY, 1967

(in thousands)

Branch of activity	Employment
Agriculture, forestry and fishing	322
Mining, quarrying and turf production	10
Manufacturing industries	201
Building and construction	73
Electricity, gas and water	12
Commerce, insurance and finance	168
Transport, communications and storage	58
Public administration and defence	45
Other non-agricultural economic activity	174
Total at work	1,063
Out of work	57
Total Labour Force	1,120

Source: *Review of 1967 and Outlook for 1968*. Dublin: Stationery Office, 1968, p. 44.

Table I–4 indicates an 'out of work' or unemployment figure of 57 thousand, a rate of about 5 per cent, for 1967; this rate is also typical for earlier years.

The source of employment by major sectors has greater meaning when compared with that of other countries. Unfortunately, lack of comparable data makes this difficult to achieve. However, one can make a rough comparison of Irish data with figures on employment derived in a study of eight countries (United States, Canada, United Kingdom, Sweden, France, Italy, India and Japan, for the early 1950's.[1] The interesting part of such a comparison is that the structure of employment for Ireland is remarkably similar to that of Japan. Although Japan is also an open economy and represents a small geographical area, her population size is considerably greater (about 95 million) than Ireland's. Compared with the other countries, with the exception of India, Ireland and Japan have relatively large agricultural sectors and small manufacturing sectors; the importance of all of the remaining sectors is somewhat more similar regardless of the country.

External commercial relations. As noted earlier, Ireland is highly dependent upon sales in foreign markets, especially of agricultural products; foreign markets are also a source of certain commodities which cannot be produced readily in the domestic

TABLE I–5
EXTERNAL TRADE BY SITC SECTION, 1967

(in millions of pounds)

SITC Section	Exports	Imports
Sect. 0 Live animals and food	£153.3	£ 59.8
Sect. 1 Drink and tobacco	9.7	9.0
Sect. 2 Raw materials except fuels	15.6	28.5
Sect. 3 Mineral fuels, lubricants, etc.	6.3	37.5
Sect. 4 Animal, vegetable oils and fats	.8	1.9
Sect. 5 Chemicals	8.4	35.8
Sect. 6 Manufactured goods	32.3	80.3
Sect. 7 Machinery and transport equipment	13.6	92.3
Sect. 8 Manufactured articles, n.e.s.	24.0	27.2
Sect. 9 Parcel post, special transactions	11.5	18.2
Total	£275.7	£390.5

Source: Central Statistics Office. *Trade Statistics of Ireland* (Year 1967 and December 1967). Dublin: Stationery Office, 1968, pp. 3-5.

economy. Unlike the larger and more self-sufficient countries, the value of Ireland's exports exceeds domestic investment, and imports exceed domestic savings; it is for this particular reason that the foreign trade sector is of strategic importance.

The composition of Ireland's merchandise exports and imports by Standard International Trade Classification (SITC) Section for 1967 is presented in Table I–5. By far the largest single category of exports is live animals and food (SITC Section 0) which accounted for £153.3 million out of a total value of all exports of £275.7 million; this is slightly more than one-half the value of all exports. The significance of agriculture as an export sector appears even greater when it is recognized that certain other SITC Sections, such as Section 1 (drink and tobacco), Section 2 (raw materials except fuels and Section 4 (animal and vegetable oils and fats) contain a highagricultural commodity content. Even SITC Section 6 (manufactured goods) includes items with a high agricultural content such as leather and leather manufactures, textile yarns and fabrics. The remaining categories of exports are relatively small, but have shown the highest rate of expansion in recent years.

Imports are divided somewhat more evenly among the ten SITC Sections. As indicated in Table I–5, the two largest import categories are SITC Section 6 (manufactured goods) and Section 7 (machinery and transport equipment). Section 0 (live animals and food) is the third most important category.

One of the crucial features of Ireland's external trade situation is its close ties with, and dependence upon, the British economy. Until 1922, Ireland was essentially a component of the U.K. commercial system. Political independence and difficulties of an economic nature led to a deterioration in commercial transactions for a time but Irish ties to Britain were not long severed. Ireland became part of the Sterling Area which gradually developed following the demise of the international gold standard. The Irish pound is pegged to the British pound and virtually all of Ireland's domestic banking and foreign exchange reserves take the form of sterling claims. The first Anglo -Irish trading agreement in 1938 amounted to a freeing of trade for certain commodities; this finally culminated in the Trade Agreement of 1965 which will lead to the establishment of a free trade area and the complete removal of trade barriers between the two countries. Labour is also free to move between the two countries under existing arrangements. The extent of the economic ties between the two countries is also apparent in trade figures. Over 70 per cent of the Republic of Ireland's exports are to Great Britain and Northern Ireland; about 50 per cent of her imports are from the same areas. The smallness of the Irish economy, in conjunction with past political ties, has led to a 'satellitic' pattern of economic growth.

Growth in the Irish economy depends to a great extent upon developments in the British economy. Prosperity in Britain creates favourable market conditions for Irish exports and also facilitates access to London capital markets. Unfortunately, the British economy has been plagued with balance of payments problems during much of the post war period. As a result of this and other factors, Britain has not always been an ideal trading partner for an economy as dependent as Ireland's.

Other aspects of the agricultural sector. The Irish economy is heavily dependent upon its agricultural sector. This dependence is reflected in data showing national income by origin, source of employment and composition of export trade. Irish agriculture is not inefficient by world standards and yet it cannot be considered even a moderately prosperous sector. Fortunes in the agricultural sector, as well as any other sector, depend not only upon conditions of supply but also those of demand. However, since much of Irish produce is sold abroad, the success of the Irish farmer hinges largely on conditions in foreign markets. According to some estimates, total real output in agriculture has not increased substantially even over the past 100 years (if adjustments are made for the additional cattle production made possible by a reduction in the use of horses).[2] Greater success might have been achieved had domestic industry expanded more rapidly or had world market conditions been more favourable. One result has been rural depopulation of a relative length and magnitude exceeding that of other industrial countries. Further, there has been no offsetting increase in the urban population; instead, emigration and other factors have led to a decline in the size of the total population.

The capacity to expand agricultural output exists; the limitation on production is more closely related to profitable market opportunities. The Irish economy appears to have a comparative advantage in various temperate-zone food products including dairy products, pigmeat and grain-derived produce. In terms of gross value of output, the major agricultural produce in 1967 (in order of importance) was: cattle and calves, milk, pigs, sheep and lambs, barley, eggs, wheat and potatoes – all of which accounted for almost 90 per cent of the gross value of agricultural output. Ireland is largely a country of small farms: three-fourths are less than 50 acres in size; one-half are less than 30. If this type of farm is to survive, adequate markets must be secured for a greater volume of various types of grain-derived produce.

The small country exporting temperate zone agriculture products faces a dilemma in that larger external markets for food and raw material products are not readily available nor can such a country shift easily to expanded shipments of industrial goods. Policies of governments of North America and Europe reflect an unwillingness to encourage a shift of domestic resources out of sectors in which they have developed a comparative disadvantage. The European Economic Community, for example, has established a variable levy system which provides complete protection to domestic producers. Regardless of how competitive the Irish farmer might be, he cannot sell in the Community market unless the demand for commodities exceeds the Community supply. Quotas established by many other countries are equally restrictive and may prevent entry of agricultural products regardless of the efficiency of the external producer. An additional factor is that the demand for most agricultural products is income inelastic; world demand for such items is growing less rapidly than for manufactured commodities.

Extensive processing of agricultural and raw material commodities in the country of origin is also subject to certain limitations. The industrial countries maintain a progression in their tariff rates according to the degree of processing of the item in question. That is, in general, the greater the extent to which a commodity is proc-

21

essed or fabricated, the higher the applicable tariff rate. A rate structure of this type discourages processing and industrialization in producing countries.

Other aspects of industry. Agricultural commodities have been the major type of export from the very beginning of modern Irish trade and production. And also from the very beginning, Irish industry, for whatever reason, has been unable to maintain a permanent stronghold with manufactured commodities in foreign markets.[3]

With partition in the 1920's, the largely agricultural southern part of the island forced its way to political independence; the six northern and somewhat more industrialized counties remained attached to the mother country. The Republic of Ireland, along with many other countries, instituted a policy of industrial self-sufficiency as early as 1932. Tariffs and quotas were employed to protect existing industries and to promote new ones. Industry also expanded as the State created industrial or commercial enterprises and supported others in which it developed a financial interest. In subsequent years, the industrial sector expanded in importance; the number of workers employed in mining, quarrying, turf production, manufacturing, construction, electricity, gas and water, increased from 200 thousand in the late 1930's, about 15 per cent of the labour force, to 296 thousand in 1967, almost 27 per cent of the labour force. The rise in the share of workers in industry has been the result of an increase in the absolute number employed in industry combined with a decrease in the absolute number in the labour force. Industry has been unable to absorb workers as rapidly as they have moved out of the agricultural sector.

Irish industry was shielded from outside competition and for many years produced largely for the domestic market, particularly the consumer goods' market. In the manufacturing field, some of the major industries (in terms of value added) include brewing, publishing and allied trades, wholesale clothing, and bread, biscuit and flour confectioneries.

The development programming which commenced in the late 1950's reflected an abrupt reversal of earlier industrial policies. The approach employed in the 1930's was to encourage industrial self-sufficiency through the use of protective tariffs which became permanent in nature and which led to production limited largely to the home market. Under the new policies, industrial sales in export markets came to be emphasized and are encouraged through the use of generous subsidies and tax concessions but under the condition that recipient firms be able to compete eventually with external firms. Many of the newer firms have a strong export orientation; this is in part the result of government tax concessions and a belief that in the long-run the export market will be a profitable one. The major manufactured exports include meat and meat preparations, dairy products, beverages, textile fibres and yarn, fabrics, clothing and footwear. In recent years, industrial exports grew more rapidly than agricultural shipments; as a share of total exports, they have expanded from 31 per cent in 1961 to 41 per cent in 1967.

Other aspects of foreign trade. The examination of foreign trade up to this point has focused on the role and nature of Irish exports. A major purpose of exports, of course, is to finance imports and it is a country's import requirements which in a fundamental way reflect the country's dependence on foreign trade.

The productive structure of the Irish economy and the nature of its dependence on foreign countries is reflected in a series of ratios which measure the 'import content of total market supplies.' Such ratios express the value of imports as a percentage of market supplies. Market supplies, in turn, are defined to include both imports and gross national product. A computation by Leser of total Irish imports and market supplies resulted in a ratio slightly under 30 per cent for the years 1947-1961.

In terms of the nature of Irish dependence on imports, Leser's breakdown by categories is of greater interest. The import content for any given category depends upon the demand for that category of items in the domestic economy combined with the capacity of the economy to produce that group of items in an economic fashion. The greater the import content, the less capable the system is of meeting domestic demands in view of the existing resource base, productive, structure, tariff system, and alternative use of resources. For the different categories for which import content ratios were computed the figures were as follows: producers' capital goods, almost 3 per cent; food, drink and tobacco, almost 2 per cent; miscellaneous consumer goods, about 7 per cent; materials for agriculture, about 1 per cent; materials for industry, almost 15 per cent; and invisibles, etc., about 7 per cent.[4] Ireland is most dependent upon external sources for materials for industry; approximately one-half of total imports were of this type.

The importance of the foreign trade sector is also reflected in the value of customs duties applied to imports. In 1967, customs duties were the most important single source of revenue (slightly more important than the income tax), providing about 25 per cent of total Exchequer revenue.

Planning and the role of government. Like many European countries, the Irish economy is 'planned' in the same sense that the government establishes targets for the main sectors and subsequently uses a variety of policies and techniques to induce an allocation of resources compatible with the specified targets. The productive capacity of the economy is largely privately owned and consumers, workers and businesses respond freely to unrestricted market forces. In general, success of Irish planning depends largely upon the willingness of the private sector to respond to guidance and assistance offered by the State. Planning is not authoritarian and becomes an integrated operation only insofar as there is widespread agreement and acceptance of the means and objectives of economic progress.

Nevertheless, the government does influence resource allocation to achieve employment, price and growth objectives through the use of monetary and fiscal policy, subsidies and direct controls. Furthermore, the State-sponsored Bodies can be directed toward the achievement of national goals with less regard for profits than the private firm.

The status of the State-sponsored Bodies, those concerns of an industrial or commercial character which have been created by the State or in which the State has a direct financial interest, differs in terms of methods of finance, legal status, and extent to which they are controlled by Parliament. The government has not followed a doctrinaire approach in the development of State-sponsored Bodies; instead, it has limited its action largely to those areas which are in the national interest and for which private enterprise has failed to assume the initiative. Some of the fields involved include central banking, electricity, railways, peat production, sugar production, airlines and steel works. In 1963, the State-sponsored Bodies with a trading or commercial function employed an estimated 50 thousand workers.

The First Programme for Economic Expansion was introduced in 1958. It marked the earliest comprehensive effort on the part of the Irish government to employ all available methods in an integrated fashion to increase the growth rate of GNP and thus reduce unemployment and emigration. Earlier reports had assessed the weakness and the potential of the Irish economy: IBEC Technical Service Corporation's *Industrial Potentials of Ireland* (1952); reports by the Capital Investment Advisory Committee (1957); and the Department of Finance's *Economic Development* (1958).

Thus after decades of unemployment, emigration and general economic stagnation in the Irish economy, the government took the position that if the economy were to participate in the growth and prosperity which characterized other European countries, deliberate and comprehensive efforts would be necessary to

24

TABLE I-6
PROJECTED SECTORAL GROWTH, 1964-1970

Sector	1963 sectoral products at 1960 prices (£ million)	Average annual rate of change 1964-1970 (per cent)	Sectoral products in 1970 at 1960 prices (£ million)
Agriculture, forestry and fishing	143.0	3.8	186.0
Industry	204.0	7.1	330.0
Other domestic (including stock appreciation adjustment)	273.0	3.6	349.0
Net foreign income	36.0	-9.4	18.0
GNP at factor cost	656.0	4.3	883.0
Indirect taxes less subsidies	96.0	4.3	130.0
GNP at market prices	752.0	4.3	1,013.0

Source: *Second Programme for Economic Expansion: A Digest.*
Dublin: Stationery Office, p. 24.

revitalize domestic agriculture, to expand domestic industry, and to make both sectors sufficiently competitive to gain greater access to world markets. Objectives of the First Programme were modest and generally the actual performance exceeded the specified objectives. In 1964, the Second Programme was launched; it was more detailed and also established targets for the major sectors. In both Programmes it was specified that the export performance of the economy would be one of the principial criteria for assessing the success of the operation. It was expected that the Third Programme would be introduced in late 1968 to cover the four years 1969-1972.

Target growth for 1970. The target growth rates for 1964-1970 for major sectors of the economy are presented in Table I-6 along with sectoral output for 1963 and 1970 (both in 1960 prices). In order that GNP increase by 50 per cent during the decade of the sixties, which is comparable to the aggregate growth target of the countries participating in the Organization for Economic Cooperation and Development, the required average annual rate of expansion would be 4.3 per cent during the period 1964-1970. Growth rates within the economy would vary from sector to

TABLE I–7
EXPORTS BY MAJOR SECTOR, 1963 AND 1966, AND PROJECTED, 1970[a]

(in millions of pounds)

Sector	1963	1966	1970
Agricultural	£109.9	109.5	157.5
Industrial	66.9	113.8	176.5
Fishing and forestry	1.9	2.3	3.0
Parcel post and temporary transactions	14.2	13.4	23.7
Total	£192.9	239.0	360.7

[a] All figures are in 1960 prices. Projections have been revised somewhat by the government from those made when the Second Programme was instituted.

Source: Córas Tráchtála (Irish Export Board). *Annual Report 1966.* Dublin: 1967, p. 7.

sector in accordance with anticipated changes in productivity and in consumer demands in domestic and foreign markets.

The agricultural, forestry and fishing sector would expand at a rate of 3.8 per cent each year. Productivity gains in this sector are expected to be greater than average for the economy so that employment, both in relative and absolute terms, would decline. The sector entitled 'other domestic' would expand at an average annual rate of 3.6 per cent each year. It is largely a service sector, including commerce, insurance, transport and communication, and public administration. Since productivity gains are typically lowest in the service sectors, the number of workers employed would have to grow by almost 2 per cent each year to achieve the target growth rate.

The highest rate of growth, an annual average rate of 7.1 per cent, has been set for industry. Growth at this rate would involve an increase in employment at an annual average rate of 2.9 per cent and in productivity of 4.1 per cent. The industry groups which are expected to develop most rapidly are chemicals and chemical products; structural clay products, glass, cement; metals and engineering; and other manufacturing industries.

Net income from foreign sources, which includes the *net* inflow from profits, wages, pensions and emigrant remittances, is expected to decline by 1970. Expansion of domestic productive capacity would lead to a reduction in holdings of foreign stocks and bonds and a greater reliance on borrowing from abroad, hence the net inflow of interest and profits will decline. In addition, if the flow of emigration is curbed, the net inflow of remittances would decrease.

Achievement of the target growth rate will lead to a greater inflow of imports to help supply the raw material and capital goods requirements of industry and the consumer demands of the population at large. This, in turn, will place unprecedented demands upon the export sector. The extent to which shipments from major sectors are expected to increase during the period 1963-1970 to facilitate the target growth in GNP is indicated in Table I-7. The value of total exports must increase from £192.9 million in 1963 to £360.7 (in 1963 prices) by 1970 to provide sufficient foreign exchange to finance required imports. The major increase, both in absolute and relative terms, would stem from the industrial sector, in which exports would rise by approximately 160 per cent during the period 1963-1970. Agricultural exports would also have to expand at a substantial rate which implies favourable market conditions in foreign countries.

Also included in Table I-7 are actual export values for 1966 (in 1960 prices). Although the growth in agricultural exports has not maintained the pace necessary to meet the 1970 target, industrial exports have expanded more than adequately to meet the 1970 requirements, assuming the 1966 trend continues. *Total* exports by 1966 were almost 5 per cent lower than the amount needed to meet target requirements at that time. It is obvious that growth targets in the export sector reflect an ambitious, yet possible programme which will require not only adequate market opportunities abroad but also an aggressive policy on the part of export establishments.

1. Joe S. Bain. *International Differences in Industrial Structure.* New Haven, Conn.: Yale University Press, 1966, pp. 13-18.
2. See Raymond D. Crotty. *Irish Agricultural Production.* Cork, Ireland: Cork University Press, 1966, p. 190. Crotty's book provides an excellent description and analysis of the economic and agricultural history of Ireland from the early 1800's through 1965.
3. Several studies have been made of Irish trade through the 1920's in an effort to determine the reasons why Irish industry failed to develop as extensively as that of Britain and countries of Western Europe. See, for example, E. J. Riordan. *Modern Irish Trade and Industry.* London: Methuen & Co., 1920.
4. C. E. V. Leser. *Imports and Economic Growth in Ireland,* 1947-1961. Dublin: The Economic Research Institute, June, 1963.

CHAPTER II

THE BALANCE OF PAYMENTS

A country's balance of payments statement is important in that it reflects the position of that country in the world economy. For this reason, the statement is frequently used as a source of information suggesting the type of monetary and fiscal policy which can and should be used to achieve both domestic and external economic objectives. A balance of payments might be defined as a statement summarizing the nature of all economic transactions between the residents (individuals, business firms, and government agencies) of one country and the residents of all other countries for a given period of time. Although there are many types of economic transactions in international commerce, they can all be included within such major categories as merchandise and service trade, short- and long-term capital flows, and unilateral transfers. The statement reflects movements or flows for a specified period of time, usually a year. It is not cumulative in nature; the statement for a given year does not show a country's *total* investment abroad, nor the *total* extent to which foreigners are investing in the country. It shows totals only for the period under consideration.

Balance of payments statistics are collected by governments from a variety of sources including returns completed by banks, insurance companies and trading concerns, and other information from exchange control agencies and customs officials. In Ireland, the statement is prepared quarterly but at annual rates. The official balance of international payments for the Republic is prepared by the Central Statistics Office and presented in the quarterly *Irish Statistical Bulletin*.

In addition to a 'global' statement which indicates aggregate transactions with the rest of the world as a unit, a statement showing the balance with different monetary areas is also prepared. In this statement, Ireland's balance of payments is presented *vis-à-vis* several different areas: Great Britain and Northern Ireland; rest of the Sterling Area; total Sterling Area; the U.S. and Canada; countries of the Organization for Economic Cooperation and Development; and all other countries. In terms of types of transactions, by far the greatest amount of detail is included in the global statement.

Description of balance of payments items. Balance of payments statistics for the years 1962-1966 are presented in Table II–1. The

TABLE II–1
ESTIMATED BALANCE OF INTERNATIONAL PAYMENTS IN THE YEARS 1962–1966

CATEGORY	Inward or Credit Movements (Exports)				
	1962	1963	1964	1965	1966
	£ thousand				
CAPITAL ITEMS:					
1. Government transactions:					
a. Changes in holdings of Trustee Savings Banks and Government Funds	2,955	—	14,784	—	1
b. Indebtedness to Government of the United States of America under European Recovery Programme	—	—	—	—	—
c. Payments to International Institutions (I.M.F., I.B.R.D., I.F.C., I.D.A.)	—	—	—	—	8,036
2. Changes in external funds of the Central Bank	—	—	—	13,851	—
3. Banking transactions – changes in net external assets	—	13,189	8,500	4,161	4,050
4. Purchases and sales of securities by private holders through Irish stockbrokers and banks	15,139	15,930	17,505	17,337	16,604
5. Movements arising out of capital issues by companies					
a. Public issues	1,200	969	3,696	838	2,156
b. Private issues	1,443	2,195	2,268	3,217	2,857
6. Net capital payments in respect of life insurance	—	—	—	—	—
7. Withdrawals from British Post Office Savings Banks	591	586	575	586	551
8. Encashment of British Savings Certificates	39	35	41	53	56
9. Other capital transactions:					
a. Extern subscriptions to Central Government or Local Authority issues, prize bonds, exchequer bills	3,501	5,630	63	2,379	18,358
b. Borrowing by Semi-State Concerns (incl. Trade Credits)	560	—	9,461	2,243	471
c. Net change in extern capital of Hire Purchase Concerns	—	1,500	2,800	2,300	30
d. Other Direct Investment by externs	14,209	12,389	18,706	11,027	14,363
e. Other transactions	5,300	5,080	2,939	2,989	8,337
Total: Capital Items	44,937	57,503	81,338	60,981	75,870
Balance on Capital Account	—	—	—	—	—

TABLE II–1
ESTIMATED BALANCE OF INTERNATIONAL PAYMENTS IN THE YEARS 1962–1966

CATEGORY	Outward or Debit Movements (Imports)				
	1962	1963	1964	1965	1966
	£ thousand				
CAPITAL ITEMS:					
1. Government transactions:					
a. Changes in holdings of Trustee Savings Banks and Government Funds	—	995	—	—	—
b. Indebtedness to Government of the United States of America under European Recovery Programme	793	817	836	1,086	1,119
c. Payments to International Institutions (I.M.F., I.B.R.D., I.F.C., I.D.A.)	246	897	586	409	3,896
2. Changes in external funds of the Central Bank	8,472	15,068	28,479	—	33,458
3. Banking transactions – changes in net external assets	3,701	—	—	—	—
4. Purchases and sales of securities by private holders through Irish stockbrokers and banks	16,127	15,272	17,537	15,133	18,619
5. Movements arising out of capital issues by companies					
a. Public issues	—	—	—	—	—
b. Private issues	—	—	—	—	—
6. Net capital payments in respect of life insurance	2,060	2,270	2,457	2,600	2,700
7. Withdrawals from British Post Office Savings Banks	—	—	—	—	—
8. Encashment of British Savings Certificates	—	—	—	—	—
9. Other capital transactions:					
a. Extern subscriptions to Central Government or Local Authority issues, prize bonds, exchequer bills	—	—	—	—	—
b. Borrowing by Semi-State Concerns (incl. Trade Credits)	—	80	—	—	—
c. Net change in extern capital of Hire Purchase Concerns	100	—	—	—	—
d. Other Direct Investment by externs	—	—	—	—	—
e. Other transactions	—	—	—	—	—
Total: Capital Items	31,499	35,399	49,895	19,228	59,792
Balance on Capital Account	13,438	22,104	31,443	41,753	16,078

TABLE II-1
ESTIMATED BALANCE OF INTERNATIONAL PAYMENTS IN THE YEARS 1962–1966

CATEGORY	Inward or Credit Movements (Exports)				
	1962	1963	1964	1965	1966
	£ thousand				
CURRENT ITEMS:					
10. Merchandise – Total exports (f.o.b.) and total imports (c.i.f.)†	164,566	186,374	212,257	211,362	234,422
11. Commission earnings of import agents	3,400	3,700	4,400	4,500	4,550
12. Coin and bullion	186	99	117	69	156
13. Transportation	5,643	5,440	8,235	8,783	12,069
14. Receipts and payments in respect of tourism and travel, etc.	45,600	49,800	58,800	67,700	65,100
15. Income from investment abroad and extern profits, etc.	33,896	34,898	38,766	44,231	45,129
16. Net outflow in respect of rental of films, etc.	—	—	—	—	—
17. Emigrants' remittances and legacies:					
a. Great Britain and the Six Counties	6,326	5,662	5,607	5,726	7,017
b. Other countries	7,384	7,449	7,865	8,789	8,164
18. Pensions and allowances:					
a. Great Britain and the Six Counties	3,920	4,070	4,450	4,700	4,650
b. Other countries	1,300	1,500	1,695	1,700	1,750
19. Payments to the British Government	—	—	—	—	—
20. Expenditure of Irish Lights Service	774	943	1,224	1,221	1,364
21. Posts, telegraphs and telephone payments and earnings	257	204	289	280	248
22. Diplomatic, consular and similar expenditure	450	480	550	600	600
23. Other known current items	9,608	10,074	11,963	15,308	15,759
24. Balance unaccounted for	11,091	12,480	7,530	5,409	12,714
Total: Current Items	294,401	323,173	363,748	380,378	413,692
Balance on Current Account	13,438	22,104	31,443	41,753	16,078

TABLE II-1
ESTIMATED BALANCE OF INTERNATIONAL PAYMENTS IN THE YEARS 1962–1966

| CATEGORY | Outward or Debit Movements (Imports) | | | | |
	1962	1963	1964	1965	1966
	£ thousand				
CURRENT ITEMS:					
10. Merchandise – Total exports (f.o.b.) and total imports (c.i.f.)	264,829	297,571	339,383	362,612	363,625
11. Commission earnings of import agents	—	—	—	—	—
12. Coin and bullion	91	177	321	361	956
13. Transportation	—	—	—	—	—
14. Receipts and payments in respect of tourism and travel, etc.	19,200	22,400	25,900	28,200	31,600
15. Income from investment abroad and extern profits, etc.	20,196	21,380	25,661	26,461	28,814
16. Net outflow in respect of rental of films, etc.	750	760	780	800	910
17. Emigrants' remittances and legacies:					
a. Great Britain and the Six Counties	—	—	—	—	—
b. Other countries	350	350	375	400	400
18. Pensions and allowances:					
a. Great Britain and the Six Counties	445	480	680	611	700
b. Other countries	83	90	89	101	102
19. Payments to the British Government	250	250	250	250	250
20. Expenditure of Irish Lights Service	—	—	—	—	—
21. Posts, telegraphs and telephone payments and earnings	426	568	390	724	453
22. Diplomatic, consular and similar expenditure	496	561	683	662	733
23. Other known current items	723	690	799	949	1,227
24. Balance unaccounted for —	—	—	—	—	—
Total: Current Items	307,839	345,277	395,191	422,131	429,770
Balance on Current Account	—	—	—	—	—

Source: Central Statistics Office. *Irish Statistical Bulletin.* June 1967, p. 75.

statement is divided into two major parts: the capital account (lines 1-9e), which shows short- and long-term lending and investment; and the current account (lines 10-24), which reflects the movement of goods and services. It will be noted that the net balance on the capital account for any given year just equals the net balance on current account for that same year.

The figures in the columns of Table II–1 on pages 29 and 31 reflect inward or credit items; they include receipts arising from merchandise and gold exports (lines 10 and 12), provision of services to foreigners (lines 11, 13, 14, 20, 21, and 22), income from foreign investments (line 15), and remittances from emigrants (line 17). Credits also arise as foreigners invest in Ireland or purchase Irish stocks and bonds (lines 4, 5 and 9), as the Irish government borrows from abroad (line 1), and as Irish residents reduce their holdings of foreign liquid assets (lines 7 and 8). Finally, credits arise as a result of a reduction in Irish banks' net external assets (lines 2 and 3) which to a great extent is the result of Irish banks reducing their deposits in external banks. Because of unknown errors and omissions in collecting and assembling the statistics, a statistical discrepancy arises, termed 'balance unaccounted for' (line 24).

The most important credit entry, or source of foreign exchange, is merchandise exports, a situation which characterizes most trading countries. Next in importance are two service accounts–receipts in respect of tourism and travel, and income from investment abroad.

Figures in the columns on pages 30 and 32 reflect outward or debit items; such payments arise as a result of merchandise, coin and bullion imports (lines 10 and 12), provision of services by foreigners to the Irish (lines 14, 16, 21, and 22), the distribution of interest and dividends of Irish firms to foreigners (line 15), annuity payments to the British government (line 19), and immigrant remittances (line 17). Debits also arise as Irish residents purchase foreign stocks and bonds or invest abroad (line 4), as loans to foreigners are repaid (lines 1b and 1c), and as Irish banks' net external reserves are increased; in general, this occurs as they expand their holdings of deposits in foreign banks (lines 2 and 3).

By far the most important debit entry, or use of foreign exchange, is merchandise imports. Other payments of a large size are for tourism and travel abroad, payment of interest and profits to foreigners, and for the purchase of foreign stocks and bonds.

For the five years covered by Table II–1, Ireland experienced a deficit on current account transactions ranging in size from £13,438 thousand in 1962 to £41,753 thousand in 1965. The current account deficit reflects an excess of merchandise imports over exports which is only partially offset by such favourable items as the service accounts. But the deficit on all current items, which must be distinguished from an over-all *balance of payments* deficit, is offset by the capital account surplus. In other words, during these years Ireland has experienced a capital account surplus with receipts on these accounts exceeding payments. The net inflow occurs as a result of two factors – foreigners investing in Ireland (new capital inflows), and Irish residents reducing their investments abroad (foreign disinvestment).

A capital account surplus characterizes Ireland's position in the world economy for most of the years since the end of World War II.

Equality of debits and credits. The nature of international transactions as reflected in the balance of payments is such that total debits must equal total credits. Thus in 1966, total credits of £489,562 thousand (£75,870 thousand on capital account plus £413,692 thousand on current account) equalled total debits of £489,562 thousand (£59,792 thousand on capital account plus £429,770 thousand on current account). This equality reflects a basic characteristic of any given international transaction, namely, that any such transaction involves both a debit (or debits) and a credit (or credits). The typical transaction, because it probably will be financed through the banking system, is likely to involve a change in the net external assets of commercial banks (line 3, Table II–1) as part of the process.

Assume, for example, that an Irish firm imports merchandise from abroad. The import itself would be included in the balance of payments as a debit (line 10). But an equal credit entry is required; in this instance it is likely that the importer reduces the amount he holds in Irish banks to accommodate payment. In exchange, the Irish banks transfer deposits they hold in London banks to the *foreign* exporter or to a bank in his country. This final transfer, which involves a reduction in the external assets of Irish commercial banks is also included in the balance of payments statement as a credit entry (line 3, Table II–1). Hence the equality of debits and credits.

Transactions of an opposite nature also occur. Thus an export of merchandise, a balance of payments credit, also necessitates an equal debit; in this instance the debit is likely to be represented by an increase in external assets of Irish commercial banks, i.e., an expansion in their deposits in London banks (line 3, Table II–1).

Long-term capital transactions are financed in much the same fashion. As an illustration, if a British resident were to purchase stocks from an Irish corporation it would appear as a credit entry (possibly line 9, Table II–1). In balance of payments terminology, this is a long-term capital inflow for Ireland, a long-term capital outflow for Britain. As the British resident pays for the stocks, there is an offsetting debit on the Irish balance of payments, possibly an increase in external assets of Irish commercial banks in London banks. In balance of payments terminology, the increase in deposits in London banks is termed a short-term capital outflow. To summarize this particular transaction, from Ireland's point of view, a long-term capital inflow (a balance of payments credit) was offset by a short-term capital outflow (a balance of payments debit). It might be added that short-term movements are defined somewhat arbitrarily to include assets or claims with a maturity of less than one year; long-term movements, a year or more.

Balance of payments deficits. It is apparent that the Irish banking system plays a key role in financing most external transactions. The deposits they hold in London banks include 'working balances,' as part of total external reserves. These deposits are both added to, and substracted from, in the normal course of business to accommodate the needs of private traders and investors. But if there is a tendency for external payments in the non-bank sector to exceed receipts over an extended period of time, the banks' deposits in London will decline and may have to be replenished by drawing on the external deposits of the Central Bank. Should these deposits and other external assets of the entire banking system decline significantly for an extended period, Ireland would be experiencing a balance of payments deficit. A deficit of this nature, which must be distinguished from a *current account* deficit, cannot persist indefinitely because the banking system has a limited volume of external reserves with which to finance the excess of outward payments. As an illustration, the net external reserves of the Irish banking system decreased by £18,012 thousand in 1965 (lines 2 and 3, Table II–1). During the following year the Irish government borrowed £8,036 thousand from the International Monetary Fund the result of which was to replenish, in part, their external assets (line 1c, Table II–1).

If there is a tendency over an extended period of time for external receipts in the non-bank sector to exceed payments, the external reserves of Irish banks will generally rise. In most instances this signifies a balance of payments surplus.

Thus a balance of payments deficit might be tentatively identified as a situation in which a country's foreign exchange reserves, which for Ireland would consist largely of external assets held by

35

TABLE II-2
BASIC GLOBAL STATEMENT, 1961-65

(in millions of U.S. dollars)

	1961 Credit	1961 Debit	1962 Credit	1962 Debit	1963 Credit	1963 Debit	1964 Credit	1964 Debit	1965 Credit	1965 Debit
A. GOODS AND SERVICES										
1. Merchandise1	740	825	738	875	814	983	940	1,116	996	1,190
	476	705	461	742	521	834	596	948	601	1,015
2. Nonmonetary gold	—	—	—	—	—	—	—	—	—	1
3. Freight2	12	—	12	—	13	—	16	—	17	—
4. Other transportation	23	10	25	12	26	13	32	14	37	15
4.1 Passenger fares	*17*	*..*	*19*	*..*	*20*	*..*	*26*	*..*	*30*	*..*
4.2. Other	*6*	*10*	*6*	*12*	*6*	*13*	*6*	*14*	*7*	*15*
5. Travel	122	46	128	54	139	63	165	73	190	79
6. Investment income	92	54	95	57	98	60	108	68	120	64
7. Government, n.i.e.	1	1	1	1	1	1	2	2	2	3
8. Other services	14	9	16	10	16	12	21	11	29	13
NET GOODS AND SERVICES	—	85	—	138	—	169	—	176	—	194
Trade balance (1 and 2)	—	229	—	281	—	313	—	352	—	415
Net services (3 through 8)	144	—	143	—	144	—	176	—	221	—
B. TRANSFER PAYMENTS	77	5	76	5	74	5	79	6	81	6
9. Private	77	2	76	2	74	2	78	3	81	3
9.1. Legacies and migrants' remittances	*39*	*1*	*38*	*1*	*37*	*1*	*38*	*1*	*41*	*1*
9.2. Other	*38*	*1*	*38*	*1*	*37*	*1*	*40*	*2*	*40*	*2*
10. Central government	—	3	—	3	—	3	1	3	—	3
NET TRANSFER PAYMENTS	72	—	71	—	69	—	73	—	75	—

	1	2	3	4	5	6	7	8	9	10
NONMONETARY SECTORS	33	—	64	—	67	—	98	—	63	—
11. Direct investment	31	—	44	—	41	—	61	—	38	—
12. Other private long-term	—	4	16	—	12	—	38	—	17	—
12.1. Liabilities	5	—	18	—	17	—	51	13	27	10
12.2 Assets	—	9	—	5	2	1	—	1	3	—
13. Other private short-term	—	—	1	—	2	—	2	—	3	—
14. Local government	11	—	5	—	12	—	—	—	5	—
15. Central government	14	—	8	—	15	—	—	—	8	—
15.1. Irish Government securities	—	2	—	2	—	2	—	—	—	—
15.2. Other liabilities	2	1	—	1	—	1	—	—	—	3
15.3. Subscriptions to IDA	1	—	—	—	—	—	—	—	—	—
MONETARY SECTORS	38	36	39	26	40	5	43	9	54	—
16. Private institutions: liabilities	38	—	39	—	40	—	43	—	56	—
16.1. Commercial banks	33	—	39	—	35	—	35	—	50	—
16.2. Hire-purchase concerns	5	—	5	—	—	—	8	—	6	—
17. Commercial banks: assets	—	55	—	49	2	—	8	11	—	38
18. Central institutions: liabilities	—	—	—	—	—	2	—	1	—	1
18.1. IMF holdings of Irish pounds	—	—	—	—	—	2	—	1	—	—
18.2. IBRD holdings of Irish pounds	1	1	1	1	1	—	1	1	—	1
18.3. IDA holdings of Irish pounds	1	—	—	—	—	—	1	—	—	—
19. Central institutions: assets	—	19	—	16	45	—	40	—	37	—
19.1. Central government holdings	—	19	8	—	3	—	41	—	—	—
19.2. Central Bank claims	—	19	—	24	42	—	80	—	39	—
19.3 Monetary gold	—	—	—	—	—	—	1	—	—	2
NET ERRORS AND OMISSIONS	16	—	29	—	38	—	14	—	2	—

1 Exports f.o.b.; imports c.i.f.

2 Insurance on merchandise (other than that included in the c.i.f. value of imports) is appropriate to item 3, but estimates are not available.

Source: International Monetary Fund. *Balance of Payments Yearbook.* Vol. 18, April, 1967.

Irish banks, are declining. A balance of payments surplus might be identified as a situation in which foreign exchange reserves are increasing. Although these definitions are essentially accurate, they need to be modified somewhat to account for gold movements and changes in a country's tranche position with the International Monetary Fund; actually, the latter two items are not particularly large for Ireland. A second consideration pertains to the adequacy of the net external asset position of Irish banks as a measure of the country's international liquidity position. These modifications are explored in Chapter III.

The IMF presentation of balance of payments statistics. The IMF, in its annual *Balance of Payments Yearbook*, presents Irish balance of payments statistics, along with those of other member countries, somewhat differently than those presented in the *Irish Statistical Bulletin* (Table II–2). The IMF publishes these statements in a standard format; accordingly, it is relatively easy to compare the statistics of one country with those of another. Since the IMF modifications are limited largely to a rearrangement of the various accounts, the combining of certain small items, and, in recent years, the conversion of values from Irish pounds to U.S. dollars at the par value of the pound, this form of presentation will be considered only in brief fashion.

Item No. 1 (Table II–2) represents the merchandise account and also the *balance of trade* (although Item No. 2, non-monetary gold, would also be included if Ireland were a major gold producer and exporter). In 1965, Ireland exported the equivalent of $996 million worth of goods and imported $1190 million worth of goods.

Items No. 3-10 include the 'invisible' transactions; this includes services and transfer payments. The total of these plus the amount in the merchandise account represent the *current account*. In 1965, Ireland had a current account deficit of $119 million. With a proper adjustment of the net error and omissions entry at the end of Table II–2, and a conversion of values from dollars to pounds, the current account deficit for each year will correspond with those indicated in the official Irish statements reproduced in Table II–1.

Items No. 11-19 represent the capital account and include both short- and long-term flows. *Monetary* gold movements are also included in this section (Item No. 19.3). The IMF divides the Capital and Monetary Gold section into two major categories: one representing the monetary sector (or banking sector) and the other, the non-monetary sector. Changes in assets of central institutions (lines 19.1, 19.2, and 19.3) are important in that they represent what the IMF identifies as changes in Ireland's international liquidity position. This again relates to balance of payments deficits and surpluses and is examined in greater detail in Chapter III.

Other statistical statements. The balance of payments statement is one of several related statistical summaries which are prepared showing the economic position of the Irish economy. The most important are the national income accounts which show the derivation and use of such aggregates as national income and gross national product (GNP). Figures from the balance of payments are a component of these statements. The figures for Ireland's national income, for example, incude the net inflow of profits, wages, salaries and emigrants' remittances from the rest of the world. The figure for GNP is also adjusted to make allowances for net expenditures by the rest of the world.

Figures from the balance of payments are also included in input-output matrices (or interindustry tables) which have been prepared for Ireland. The input-output tables show the interrelationship of each industry with all other industries in terms of purchases (inputs) and sales (outputs). Imports are included as inputs for domestic sectors except for finished goods for direct sale to final buyers which are allocated to final demand. Exports are treated as outputs accruing to the final demand sector. As might be suggested by Table I–5 in Chapter I, the input coefficients for imports for Irish industries are highest for the metal, engineering, vehicle and other manufacturing industries; the highest outputs with respect to exports are from the agricultural and food processing sectors.[1] Because of the relatively small size of the Irish economy, the interdependency of sectors within the economy is less, and the general dependency on imports as inputs for the economy is higher, than for a large country.[2]

1. For an analysis of an Irish matrix which identifies nine industrial groups, see R. C. Geary. 'Towards an Input-Output Decision Model for Ireland,' *Statistical and Social Inquiry Society of Ireland.* Vol. XXI, Part II, pp. 67-115.
2. An examination of the various ways which imports can be treated in an input-output model for a small open economy, see J. McGilvray. 'The Stability of Coefficients in an Irish Inter-Industry Model,' *Journal of the Statistical and Social Inquiry Society of Ireland.* Volume XXI, Part III, pp. 44-70.

CHAPTER III

THE RATE OF EXCHANGE AND FOREIGN EXCHANGE RESERVES

Although economic transactions between countries are fundamentally the same as those within a country, one major difference is that the former involves the use of two monetary units and also two prices (the price of the commodity being exchanged and the price of the foreign currency or of foreign exchange in general). The price of a foreign currency or foreign exchange in terms of the domestic currency represents what is termed the rate of exchange.

Foreign exchange itself is a collective term used to identify various types of negotiable liquid claims expressed in terms of a foreign money. Foreign exchange is usually defined to include foreign currency, deposits in foreign banks, acceptances, drafts, treasury bills and other short-term assets.

Types of exchange rates. At a given moment of time, several rates of exchange may prevail reflecting the value relationship between any two currencies. The *official* or *par* rate is a fixed rate selected for stabilization purposes and expresses the value of the currency in terms of gold or U.S. dollars in accordance with provisions of the Articles of Agreement of the International Monetary Fund (IMF). The par value of the Irish pound is 14.6 units per troy ounce of gold. Alternatively, one Irish pound equals $2.40.

The *spot* rate might be thought of as the current market rate; this rate moves freely, reflecting market forces of demand and supply, but is pegged by a government agency to a range within 1 per cent above and 1 per cent below the official rate. For the Irish trader, all transactions in sterling occur at parity since the two currencies have an identical official value. Irish exchange rates for other currencies change with sterling rates for these currencies. Ireland's situation is similar to that of many other small economies which keep their currencies rigidly pegged to one of the reserve currencies – the pound sterling, the dollar or the franc.

Long, *forward*, or *time* rates, or rates for future delivery, exist when buyers and sellers of foreign exchange engage in 'hedging' to avoid the risk and uncertainty of an adverse movement in the rate of exchange; it involves the purchase or the sale of foreign exchange with the transaction to be consumated at some specified future date.

If comprehensive exchange controls are employed by a country, a *black market* rate, reflecting illegal transactions, will usually exist along with the official controlled rate. Some countries, especially under-developed ones, employ *multiple* exchange rates, the applicable rate depending upon the nature of the transaction being financed.

Irish exchange transactions. The Irishh foreign trader and investor is less conscious of a rate of exchange and the use of foreign exchange because of the nature of Ireland's relationship with Britain and because over half of Ireland's merchandise trade is with that country. The identical value of the British and the Irish pound, the circulation of a significant amount of British currency in Ireland, and the extensive holdings of deposits of Irish banks in British banks creates a situation in which for all appearances transactions between the two countries are the same as within Ireland. This is a false impression, however, for the deposits of Irish banks in British banks or other sterling claims represent foreign exchange, the amount of which rises as Ireland exports or becomes a recipient of capital inflows, and falls as Ireland imports or invests abroad.

The two-price characteristic of international transactions will become increasingly apparent to Irish traders if an increased share of trade develops with countries other than the United Kingdom and the Sterling Area. Thus an Irish importer, for example, may need to know not only the franc price of French perfume but also the pound price of francs.

By virtue of its membership in the Sterling Area (described in Chapter IV), and more specifically, because Irish banks hold a large volume of external assets in the form of deposits in London banks or other sterling assets, and because the British pound is more widely known and accepted than the Irish pound, Irish international transactions, even outside the Sterling Area, are accommodated by London banks. Thus an Irish bank draws down its British deposit to acquire francs (i.e., deposits in French banks) which are in turn sold to Irish importers of French commodities. The Irish bank expands its deposits in London banks as it sells Deutsch Marks (in London) which it had previously purchased from an Irish firm exporting to Germany. The deposits in London banks, an important form of foreign exchange, are utilized in most of Ireland's external transactions.

Determinants of the rate of exchange. The rate of exchange, like other prices, is determined by the forces of supply and demand. Foreign exchange is demanded in the market by domestic residents (individuals, business firms and governments) who wish to import goods and services, who wish to purchase foreign stocks and bonds (i.e., invest abroad) or who wish to make donations to foreigners.

The supply of foreign exchange arises as residents export commodities abroad, as they sell stocks and bonds to foreigners (i.e., a capital inflow), and as they become recipients of gifts from abroad. The equilibrium rate of exchange is that rate which equates the amount of exchange demanded with that supplied. A change in either demand or supply is likely to lead to a movement in the rate of exchange. Serving as intermediaries in the exchange market are commercial banks and foreign exchange dealers; generally the gap between the buying and the selling rate is narrow and the intermediaries rely on a large volume of transactions to make an adequate profit. However, when extensive exchange controls are in existence, the intermediary function is performed, at least in part, by a government agency .

Behaviour of the rate of exchange. The behaviour of the rate of exchange depends upon the structure of the foreign exchange market and the institutional arrangements which surround it. The exchange rate may be fixed or stable (held within a narrow range) through stabilization funds, exchange controls, or under an international gold standard. Or it may be permitted to rise or fall within an almost unlimited range in which case it is termed a freely fluctuating exchange rate.

Most of the major trading countries were on a form of the international gold standard during the last half of the nineteenth and early part of the twentieth century. Each country defined its currency in terms of gold, currencies were redeemable in gold, gold could be freely exported and imported in settlement of transactions and each country held its domestic banking reserves in the form of gold. The net result of these arrangements was that the market rate of exchange was stabilized within a narrow range known as the gold import and export points. Nations were forced to abandon the gold standard in the period between the two world wars. The immediate cause was the depletion of gold stocks which created monetary problems for some countries. However, more fundamentally it related to structural changes developing in the world economy – the disturbance of the pattern of multilateral trade which characterized the pre-World War I period. This disturbance in turn was the result of an emergence of new industrial powers as well as a new unwillingness on the part of governments to require internal economies to adjust to external conditions.

Some countries adopted freely fluctuating exchange rates for a period of time following the demise of the gold standard. Unfortunately, unstable economic conditions within nations contributed to uncertainty in exchange markets and to large, erratic movements of capital between countries. Because of presumed exchange rate instability and the lack of certainty afforded international traders and investors caused by these freely fluctuating exchange rates, most governments have employed exchange controls or stabilization funds to achieve exchange rate stability.[1]

Governments may employ exchange controls not only to establish a fixed rate of exchange, but also to regulate the composition of exports and imports and to prevent capital movements out of the country. If controls are comprehensive in nature they supplant the free exchange market; exporters and other recipients of foreign exchange must sell their receipts to the specified government agency in exchange for local currency. The exchange authorities, in turn, become the sole source of foreign exchange which is available to importers and other users of foreign exchange at a price and under conditions which the authorities deem compatible with the achievement of other domestic objectives.

When a country's rate of exchange is determined fundamentally by free market forces, which is the case under freely-fluctuating exchange rates, under an international gold standard or under stabilization funds, the value of its currency is maintained at a realistic rate in the exchange markets of the world. Such a currency can be bought and sold without restriction to cover most transactions and is said to be 'convertible'. When the currencies of most major trading countries are convertible or can be exchanged freely, a 'multilateral' trading system exists. Since a bilateral balancing of accounts between pairs of countries is not required, currency convertibility is conducive to a high level of world trade. For example, in a multilateral system, Ireland might use a net favourable external balance acquired from transactions with Great Britain and Northern Ireland to offset an unfavourable balance with any other country or countries; it is not necessary that the value of Ireland's receipts from a country just equal payments to that same country. The major advantage of such a system is that it enables exporters to sell in high-price markets and importers to buy in low-price markets regardless of the country; in the absence of a multilateral clearing system, governments might be forced to direct trade through bilateral channels and the most advantageous market opportunities may not be open to traders.

When a country imposes exchange controls, the rate of exchange is arbitrarily determined and will normally not approximate the free market rate. When the rate of exchange is fixed under these circumstances, the value of the currency in question is not realistic; it becomes over-valued (or in some circumstances under-valued) in the exchange markets. Such a currency is not freely exchanged for others and is said to be 'inconvertible'.

Comprehensive exchange controls are used by many low-income countries to affect the composition of trade and thus promote internal growth. Their currencies become inconvertible, they are usually over-valued in world markets, and the system is incompatible with a world-wide system of multilateral trade. Exchange controls may be advantageous for a country, or they may prove to be disadvantageous. But the feasibility of exchange controls is a part of a much broader question: which is most conducive to the best allocation of scarce resources – a laissez-faire, free market economy, or one in which economic decision-making is in the hands of a centralized government agency? It is generally believed that government interference with free market forces is most suitable in instances where social costs greatly diverge from private costs.

Stabilization operations. The major trading countries, at least since the late 1950's, have employed stabilization funds to confine exchange rate movements to a narrow range. The stabilization agency possesses an inventory of gold or foreign currencies and of domestic currency. A rate of exchange is selected which hopefully approximates the free market, long-run equilibrium rate. Most transactions occur through normal commercial channels in response to the needs of private traders and investors. Operations of the stabilization agency occur only occasionally to keep the rate within a range close to the official rate. If the price of the foreign currency rises above a designated point, the agency proceeds to sell foreign currency against domestic currency; if the rate falls below a certain level, it uses domestic currency to purchase foreign exchange.

The most that the stabilization agency can expect to accomplish is to even out short-run fluctuations. If the price of foreign currencies, or the rate of exchange, tends to fall persistently, the agency can continue operations by increasing its holdings of gold and foreign currencies, assuming of course that it has unlimited access to local currency. If the agency's exchange reserves along with those of the central and commercial banks continue to increase, the country would be experiencing a balance of payments surplus. If, in contrast, there is a persistent tendency for the rate of exchange to rise, operations of the stabilization agency may be hampered since normally the agency possesses a limited amount of gold and foreign currencies which can be made available for sale. If the agency's exchange reserves along with those of domestic banks tend toward depletion, the country is said to be experiencing a balance of payments deficit. To cope with a persistent tendency for the rate of exchange to rise, the stabilization agency can deplete domestic reserves of gold and foreign exchange and it might secure additional reserves through borrowing from the IMF or from some other source abroad. If these alternatives do not exist, the deficit country must permit the rate to rise above the pre-established level or else resort to exchange controls or other restrictive trade practices.

Balance of payments equilibrium. Balance of payments equilibrium prevails for the country employing stabilization funds when there is no tendency for external reserves to rise or to fall over an extended period. Alternatively, equilibrium exists when payments and receipts involving *autonomous* transactions are equal. Autonomous transactions are those undertaken for their own sake, for the profit or the satisfaction they provide the transactor. When payments and receipts of this type are equal, there is no net change in external reserves. When the value of payments and receipts differs, *induced* transactions, those not undertaken for their own sake, but to finance the transactions of other groups, lead to a change in holdings of exchange reserves.

As described earlier a large share of the banking system's external holdings is used to accommodate the autonomous transactions of the private trader and investor. These holdings are constantly being added to and subtracted from as the system facilitates the flow of commerce. But when autonomous receipts exceed autonomous payments, induced transactions lead to an increase in external reserves – a balance of payments surplus. When receipts fall short of payments, induced transactions lead to a decline in reserves as the banking system accommodates the needs of traders. If the fall in reserves continues, the country is experiencing a balance of payments deficit.

When a country experiences balance of payments disequilibrium, certain adjustments (examined in Chapter V) occur through *changes* in domestic income, prices or the rate of exchange. When the rate of exchange is held constant, changes in prices and income eventually restore equilibrium, but until this occurs, external reserves are required (assuming a balance of payments deficit) to bridge the gap between autonomous receipts and autonomous payments. Since the governments of most countries find it desirable to stabilize their exchange rates, they remain concerned with the adequacy of their external reserve holdings to finance balance of payments deficits.

International liquidity. The ability of a country to withstand a balance of payments deficit or for autonomous payments to exceed autonomous receipts without resorting to quantitative trade restrictions depends upon its holdings of liquid, negotiable assets or claims against foreign countries. Such assets are termed external reserves or international liquidity. The IMF, in its publication *International Financial Statistics* defines the concept 'international liquidity' to include three categories of assets which might be held by a country: foreign exchange, gold and Reserve Positions in the Fund. Foreign exchange, in turn, is defined by the IMF as holdings by monetary authorities (central banks, currency boards, exchange stabilization funds, and Treasury holdings to the extent that they perform stabilization operations) of bank deposits, Treasury bills, short- and long-term government securities and similar items when denominated in convertible currencies (lines 1a and 2, Table II–1).

Reserve Positions in the Fund are amounts which a deficit country can borrow from the IMF almost automatically under the Gold Tranche policy; normally, this is equal to the country's quota less the Fund's holdings of its currency (described in the following chapter), if the amount is positive. The amount held by a given country in the Reserve Position is reduced as the country draws from the Fund, and increased as other countries draw its currency.

Gold holdings, the third type, represent that amount held by a country for monetary purposes.

Irish liquidity position. The composition of Ireland's international liquidity position as defined by the IMF is shown in Table III–1 for select years 1958 through 1967. The greatest share of the total takes the form of foreign exchange; at the end of 1967, it represented almost 92 per cent of the total. Ireland's Reserve Position in the Fund stood at zero at the end of 1966; this was the result of her borrowing from the Fund earlier in the year. However, at the end of 1967, Ireland's Reserve Position amounted to the equivalent of $11 billion; this was the result of the Fund's sale of Irish currency to other countries (in this case, India and Burma) during the year.

The composition of Ireland's external liquidity position is considerably different from the aggregate of all members of the IMF. At the end of 1967, total liquidity for member countries was valued at $ 72.2 billion. Of this total about 56 per cent took the form of gold; 36 per cent, foreign exchange; and 8 per cent, Reserve Positions in the Fund. Comparatively speaking, Ireland's foreign exchange holdings were high; her gold holdings, low. Another difference relates to the composition of foreign exchange. About three-fourths of aggregate foreign exchange holdings of all IMF members were dollar claims or claims against the U.S. The remainder were claims against sterling and other convertible cur-

TABLE III–1
VALUE AND COMPOSITION OF IRISH INTERNATIONAL LIQUIDITY FOR SELECT YEARS, 1958-1967

(in millions of U.S. dollars)

Year	Gold	Reserve Position in Fund	Foreign exchange	Total	Liquidity ratio[a]
1958	18	4	283	305	55%
1960	18	8	298	324	51
1962	18	8	333	359	47
1964	19	11	416	446	46
1966	23	0	471	494	47
1967	25	11	403	439	41

[a]Ratio of reserves to annual imports.
Source: International Monetary Fund. *International Financial Statistics* (various issues). Washington, D.C.

rencies. Virtually all of Ireland's foreign exchange on the other hand represented claims against sterling.

Actually the fact that Irish banks hold deposits in British banks and other claims against sterling of such a magnitude means that Ireland is a net lender to Britain on short-term account. Similarly, other countries possessing large sterling or dollar claims are net lenders to Britain or the U.S. These are currencies or claims maintained for reserve purposes and typically the reserve countries are net short-term borrowers. The increased volume of short-term claims held against the U.S. and Great Britain by other countries is actually the result of the balance of payments deficits experienced by the two reserve currency countries during the past several years.

Although reserve currency countries are borrowers on short-term account, they are usually net lenders on long-term account. Many countries, such as Ireland, require negotiable, liquid assets for international reserves and for domestic banking reserves. At the same time, such countries need access to external resources to expand domestic productive capacity. Under such circumstances, these countries are likely to be net creditors on short-term account, net debtors on long-term account. Insofar as their reserve holdings are in the form of long-term securities, these are usually government obligations which are considered safe and which can be easily converted to a liquid asset.

During the period 1958 through 1967, Ireland's reserves increased by $134 million or about 44 per cent. Although there are no precise standards which can be employed to determine the adequacy of this increase, some criteria can be applied to determine, in a very general way, the vulnerability of Ireland's position to adverse conditions in world commerce. One criterion involves a comparison of the growth in Ireland's reserves with the growth in world reserves during the same period. While Ireland's reserves increased about 44 per cent, aggregate reserves of all IMF member countries expanded only about 25 per cent. Actually, during this same period (1958-1967), there was a significant shift in holdings of reserves of many other countries; reserves of several of the industrialized countries of Europe doubled while those of the U.S. *decreased* by about one-third.

A second way in which the adequacy of a country's reserves can be measured is through a comparison of such reserves with the value of the country's annual imports. The rationale for the comparison is that reserves are needed by the country to continue importing in event of balance of payments problems. The ratio of Ireland's reserves to its imports is also presented in Table III-1. On the basis of this ratio, it would appear that Ireland's liquidity position had deteriorated somewhat during the period, dropping from about 55 per cent in 1958 to about 41 per cent in 1967. Stated in another fashion, Ireland's liquidity position would have supported the purchase of 6.6 months' worth of imports in 1958; 4.9 months' worth in 1967.

It must be emphasized that no single measure can accurately assess the adequacy of a country's reserve position. For example, a country's reserves might be reduced somewhat as a result of increased imports of capital goods and equipment; if the net result is to modernize the country's productive capacity and make it more competitive in world markets, the country would be in a stronger position than previously. A situation in which declining reserves must be considered serious might exist if it is the result of domestic price inflation and a consequent fall in exports and rise in imports.

The adequacy of the size and the growth of reserves must also be considered in relation to the size and growth of external obligations. This is particularly true of the obligations created by the inflow of long-term investment and the subsequent servicing of the debt. The probability of a balance of payments crisis as a result of being over-burdened with fixed external obligations is examined in Chapter VII.

Problems of defining reserves. Foreign exchange is included by the IMF as one of the three components in its measurement of international liquidity. It might appear that the term foreign exchange is a straight-forward one which can be readily defined or identified in a way acceptable for a variety of purposes. Unfortunately, this is not the case. Foreign exchange is defined by the Fund to include a variety of external assets held by monetary authorities (central banks, currency boards, exchange stabilization funds and, under certain circumstances, Treasuries). The Fund's concept of foreign exchange may be adequate as a quick and ready measure of one of the components of a country's international liquidity position, but it is by no means the only way the concept can be defined.

When the IMF calculates the foreign exchange component of Ireland's liquidity position, it does not include net external assets of Irish associated or commercial banks (line 3, Table II–1) and the banks, of course, do hold assets to accommodate foreign trade. The value of net external assets (total foreign assets minus total foreign liabilities) of the commercial banks is quite large; during many years it has exceeded assets of the Central Bank. Thus the Fund's approach is a conservative one since the value of Ireland's foreign exchange is considerably greater if the net holdings of commercial banks are included. However, the Fund's approach can be justified on grounds that international liquidity should include only that foreign exchange which can be readily mobilized by the official monetary authorities in event of a balance of payments deficit. Technically speaking, reserves of commercial banks are not necessarily readily available to the Central Bank. As noted later, however, certain transactions between the Central Bank and the associated banks cause changes in the external asset position of the former and may not reflect a change in the economy's balance of payments position.[2]

Finally, the IMF's definition of international liquidity includes holdings of *long-term* securities issued by foreign governments. It might be argued that long-term bonds are not sufficiently liquid to be most useful in event of a balance of payment crisis. Long-term securities are considered somewhat illiquid because they are not always readily convertible into money without a loss occurring to the seller. Accordingly, as far as this particular aspect is concerned, the IMF's definition of reserves is not a conservative one.

The possibility of alternative definitions of external reserves or liquidity creates a serious problem in attempting to assess the strength of a country's balance of payments position. This difficulty can be illustrated with reference to the change in Ireland's position during the period 1958-1966. According to the IMF's definition of international liquidity, Ireland's external reserves increased approximately 60 per cent between 1958 and 1966. But if a broader definition of external reserves is used in order to include net external assets the increase amounted to only 22 per cent. The reason is that during this period the net external assets of commercial banks decreased by about 18 per cent. Thus it could be stated that Ireland's reserves increased either by 22 per cent or 60 per cent depending upon the choice of definitions.

The second concept of external reserves is important because it reflects the one used frequently in official Irish pronouncements on the well-being of the nation. However, rather than necessarily being related to the external liquidity position of the economy, it is simply included as a statement entitled 'External Assets of the Banking System and of Department Funds'.

The choice of definitions to express Ireland's reserve position is arbitrary and it is not realistic to assume that one is more suitable than others. Perhaps a solution might be to present figures for the two approaches simultaneously along with an explanation as to the difference.

In order to appreciate the difficulty of developing a single definition which is acceptable for all purposes, it is necessary to understand the composition of such reserves and also the factors or forces which cause their value or volume to change over time. These factors are of particular importance to the policy-maker who must use reserve figures as a basis for determining appropriate monetary and fiscal action.

Functions of Ireland's exchange assets. In order to be suitable for financing a balance of payments deficit, exchange reserves must be in a liquid form, capable of being readily mobilized, and generally acceptable as a medium of payment in the world economy. At least two of the assets described, gold and Reserve Positions with the Fund, obviously meet these conditions. The nature and composition of other assets held by the banking system must be examined to determine: (i) if they are equally useful for covering a balance of payments deficit and (ii) if changes in their volume over time are an accurate gauge of the economy's external reserve position.

Initially, it must be recognized that the banking system's external assets serve several functions which, in turn, influence their composition. External assets are maintained not only to finance balance of payments deficits, but also for at least three other purposes: as working balances to facilitate commercial transactions; as interest-earning assets for the banking system; and as reserves against domestic monetary liabilities. Reserves for financing deficits must be at least partially in the form of highly liquid assets and might include current and deposit accounts in foreign banks and possibly short-term government securities (government bills.) They must also be denominated in terms of a convertible currency, as sterling, U.S. dollars, or any one of several European currencies.

Reserves held as working balances (described in Chapter II) or to accommodate the normal purchase and sale transactions generally are in the form of current accounts in foreign banks.

External assets also take the form of interest earning investments; these are less liquid than current and deposit accounts and government bills, but typically earn a higher rate of return. Such assets might include long- and medium-term government securities; they provide a relatively high rate of return and are not immediately available for financing a balance of payments deficit. However, they can be converted into liquid assets within a reasonable period of time and without loss to the holder should the need arise.

Finally, external assets are held as a reserve against domestic bank liabilities since legal tender notes are issued by the Central Bank in exchange for certain external assets. The form of such assets is specified by law to include gold, British legal tender, bank drafts payable at sight in London, and British government securities. Because of domestic confidence in the Irish pound, these reserves are not likely to be called upon and thus need not be in highly liquid form. Accordingly, they can be in a form which also provides a relatively high rate of return for the holder.

External assets of the banking system. Because external assets perform several functions, it is necessary that they be heterogeneous with respect to maturity date, degree of liquidity, and nature of the debtor. The different types of external assets of the Irish banking system and of Departmental funds vary considerably with respect to these factors. At the end of March, 1967, they were valued at £267 million; of this total, assets of the Central Bank amounted to £165 million; net external assets of the associated banks amounted to £101 million; assets of Departmental Funds totalled slightly less than £1 million.

Assets of the Central Bank are included in the *Legal Tender Note Fund* and the *General Fund*. External assets of the two Funds are indicated in Table III–2 for 31 March, 1967. *External* reserves of the Legal Tender Note Fund, which are maintained as part of the 'backing' or 'cover' for Irish currency outstanding, represent about 70 per cent of total assets in the Fund, the remainder being domestic assets. The fact that in recent years certain types of domestic assets could be utilized for cover purposes has made a greater volume of external assets legally available for other purposes, including that of financing a balance of payments deficit. External holdings are largely in the form of British govern-

TABLE III-2
EXTERNAL ASSETS OF THE CENTRAL BANK, 31 MARCH, 1967

(in thousands of pounds)

Type of asset	Value
(a) Legal Tender Note Fund:	
Gold	2,646
British Government securities	67,420
Sterling balances on current or deposit account at the London Agency or any Bank in G.B. or Northern Ireland	132
Currency and securities of the U.S. Government	10,277
Total External Assets	**80,475**
(b) General Fund:	
British Government Securities	79,837
Other external government securities	4,577
Total External Assets	**84,414**
Aggregate External Assets: Both Funds	164,889

Source: Figures derived from Central Bank. *Report of the Central Bank of Ireland for the Year Ended 31 March 1967*. Dublin: 1967, pp. 73-75.

ment securities, although a fairly significant share is in the form of U.S. dollar claims. Both types of claims, of course, are suitable for reserve purposes. Such highly liquid assets as gold and deposits in external banks represent a small share of the total.

The external assets of the Central Bank held in the General Fund are also included in Table III-2; they also represent about 70 per cent of total assets maintained in this Fund, the remainder being domestic assets. The General Fund is utilized by the Bank as a basis for over-all monetary control, particularly discount operations. British government securities again represent the major type of external asset.

The external assets of the Central Bank generally decline as Ireland's autonomous payments exceed receipts (a balance of payments deficit) and as the Central Bank in conjunction with the associated banks perform a residual role of making foreign exchange available to traders. Actually, for most of the post-World War II years, Ireland's autonomous receipts have exceeded pay-

TABLE III–3
EXTERNAL ASSETS AND LIABILITIES OF
ASSOCIATED BANKS, MARCH QUARTER, 1967*

(in thousands of pounds)

Assets	Value
Balances with London Agents and other Banks	36,955
Money at Call and Short Notice	25,194
Bills	3,572
Loans and advances	80,416
Investments (Government)	123.559
Other assets	14,865
Total Assets	**284,561**
Liabilities	
Current accounts	92,499
Deposit accounts	72,930
Other liabilities	33,736
Total liabilities	**199,165**
Net External Assets	**£ 85,396**

*Averages of monthly figures for January, February and March 1967.

Source: Figures derived from Central Bank. *Report of the Central Bank of Ireland for the Year Ended 31 March 1967.* Dublin: 1967, p. 106.

ments (including both current account and non-bank capital account transactions) and as a result the Bank's foreign assets have expanded. However, an analysis of the Central Bank's external assets suggests certain problems associated with the use of changes in such assets as the sole indicator of trends in a country's balance of payments position or of its international liquidity position. For one thing, the aggregate value of these assets is affected by domestic as well as external factors. As a result, changes in their value need not reflect necessarily a change in Ireland's balance of payments position. Certain types of transactions between the Central Bank and the associated banks lead to changes in the former's external asset position. As an illustration, when the Central Bank issues currency to the associated banks, it acquires external assets in exchange and as a result its holdings rise. Other factors may cause a *decrease* in external assets; during the first three months of 1967, assets declined by £2.7 million as a result of transactions with commercial banks involving a decrease in domestic currency in circulation and a decrease in commercial banks' deposits with the Central Bank. This type of problem suggests the major weakness of the definition of international liquidity used by the IMF. If external reserves of the *system* as a whole are used as an indicator of Ireland's liquidity position, this problem does not arise, since those reserves lost or gained by the Central Bank would be gained or lost by the associated banks.

Use of the external position of Irish *associated banks* as an indicator of the economy's reserve position is also fraught with difficulties. The position of the associated banks of the Republic is complex because they do banking business in Northern Ireland, a different political entity, and because they hold a large share of their assets abroad. Thus the balance sheet assets and liabilities of associated banks of the Republic are divided between those held 'within the state' and those held 'elsewhere'. It is the difference between assets held elsewhere (external assets) and liabilities held elsewhere (external liabilities) which gives rise to the figure for 'net external assets'.

The net external reserve position of the associated banks for the first quarter of 1967 is indicated in Table III–3. (Figures in Table III–3 represent averages for the three months.) While net reserves amounted to about £ 85 million, gross external reserves were valued at almost £ 285 million. It might be argued, of course, that *gross* rather than *net* foreign assets of the commercial banks is a more meaningful expression of their external position. Obviously, the net position is a more conservative one. Again, however, it is not meaningful to argue that one expression is better than the other; it is far more important to understand what each entails.

The net external assets of associated banks represent a differential or an accounting identity whose assigned value will rise (fall) as external assets increase (decrease) or as external liabilities decrease (increase). Generally, net reserves fall as autonomous payments exceed autonomous receipts, and rise as such receipts fall short of payments. However, as was true with Central Bank external assets, those of the associated banks also change as a result of domestic factors and accordingly need not serve as an accurate guide to the country's external position. One such change might occur, for example, if the associated banks needed to acquire currency from the Central Bank for their customers and were to relinquish external assets in payment.

As indicated by Table III–3, a larger share of the assets of the associated banks is in the form of highly liquid assets (including

54

deposits in external banks and money at call and short notice) than is the case with the Central Bank. The greater liquidity of the associated banks reflects their holdings of working balances to accommodate the normal commercial activity of world trade and investment as well as their holdings of liquid assets to cover a potential shortage of current payments over current receipts. Their assets represent the first line of defense in the event of balance of payments problems. Although the associated banks hold liquid assets, as indicated in Table III–3, they also hold a substantial volume of investment securities, Government bonds and loans and advances. However, because the net external position is simply a differential between assets and liabilities, it is not meaningful to specify a precise ratio of either liquid or illiquid assets. Such a ratio might be compiled only with respect to gross reserves. External liabilities of the associated banks (current and deposit accounts) are largely those held by banks in Northern Ireland.

Reserves: summary and conclusions. At the end of March, 1967, Ireland's external reserves amounted to about £267 million if *net* external assets of the associated banks are included. This represents the equivalent of about 8 months' imports. Because of inter-bank transactions, *changes* in external assets of the *system* may be better indication of Ireland's reserve position than the assets of *either* the Central Bank *or* of associated banks. But the *net* nature of external assets of associated banks reduces the value of the aggregate figure. A large share of the assets is in liquid form, although a meaningful ratio cannot be specified because of the net nature of the associated banks' position.

Ireland's reserves have expanded during most years since 1948, but during those few years when declines did occur (1951, 1955, 1956 and 1965) the decline was quite substantial. Because of substantial holdings of external reserves, the Irish pound has been maintained at a one-to-one ratio with sterling by Irish banks without the use of a formalized stabilization agency. On balance, these factors would suggest that Ireland's external asset position is not a weak one.

But the nature of international finance and commerce is too complex to permit such a simple statement. The adequacy of external assets depends upon more than their absolute volume, their rate of growth or their composition. An important consideration, for example, is the extent to which future obligations are being accumulated as a result of capital inflows and the way in which the inflow is being utilized. These factors affect the possibility that reserves may have to be drawn down in the future. Thus an examination of the current account deficit and use of capital inflows is also necessary (Chapter VII).

More important, however, is that for balance of payments purposes, the adequacy of external reserves depends upon the length and magnitude of a balance of payments deficit. And these, in turn, depend upon the willingness and capacity of the government and the economy to apply restrictive fiscal and monetary measures to affect prices and incomes, or to alter the rate of exchange in such a way as to affect prices and incomes and thus keep the balance of payments under control (examined in Chapter V). Such measures cannot be easily applied because of a possible adverse impact on domestic income and employment. In addition, the openness of the Irish economy makes it difficult for the Central Bank to affect the supply of domestic credit and money.

Net external assets and the supply of money. External commerce has a direct influence on the domestic supply of money. All other things remaining equal, the quantity of money (currency and current accounts) rises as autonomous receipts from foreigners exceed autonomous payments to foreigners; the quantity of money decreases as autonomous payments exceed autonomous receipts.

Assume as an illustration that an Irish resident makes a payment to a foreigner (for the purchase of goods, services, securities or any other reason). To pay for the import, the Irish resident buys foreign exchange from a bank; as a result his current account at the bank is reduced. The bank, in turn, will experience a reduction in an asset, foreign exchange, and a reduction in a liability, a current account. Thus the quantity of money is reduced by the amount of the external payment.

A receipt transaction has the opposite effect on the quantity of money. If an Irish resident receives foreign exchange in payment for an export of goods and services, or sale of securities to foreigners, he will sell the foreign exchange to his bank and in turn acquire an addition to his current account. The bank acquires an asset, foreign exchange, as well as a liability in the form of a current account. Thus the quantity of money is increased by the amount of the external receipt.

During any given period of time, there will be many receipt transactions which serve to expand the quantity of money, and many payment transactions which contract it. Accordingly, the possibility of a *net* change in the quantity of money will depend upon the *net* impact of external transactions. All other things remaining equal, if aggregate autonomous receipts exceed aggregate payments, the quantity of money will rise; if they fall short of payments, the quantity of money will decline.

In addition, as described in an earlier section, an excess of auton-

TABLE III-4
CHANGES IN THE SUPPLY OF MONEY, 1957-1967

(in million of pounds)

Type of money	31 Dec.	31 Dec.	Change during
	1957	1967	period
Notes and coins	£ 82.3	£124.4	£ 42.1
Current accounts	116.3	234.4	118.1
Total	£198.6	£358.8	£160.2
Factors accounting for change			
Domestic credit outstanding	£202.8	£463.9	£261.1
Deposit accounts	— 190.2	— 384.3	— 194.1
Other internal assets (net)	— 3.9	— 15.1	— 11.2
External assets	189.9	294.3	104.4
Total	£198.6	£358.8	£160.2

Source: Central Bank of Ireland. *Report of the Central Bank of Ireland for the Year Ended 31 March 1966*. Dublin: 1966, pp. 66-67. Central Bank of Ireland. *Quarterly Bulletin* (February 1968) Dublin: 1968, p. 13.

omous receipts over payments results in an increase in the external assets of the banking system. If autonomous receipts fall short of payments during a given period of time, external assets of the banking system decline.

The relationship between changes in net external assets and the supply of money is crucial to an understanding of monetary developments in the Irish economy. Changes in the supply of money can be almost completely accounted for by changes in three factors; domestic credit creation, deposit accounts (a 'near money'), and net external assets. When banks extend credit, money is created; when loans are repaid, current accounts are drawn down and the supply of money is reduced. In addition, as holders of current accounts switch to deposit or savings accounts, the supply of money is lowered; or, a change from the holding of deposit to current accounts results in an increase in the supply of money.

Monetary control and external factors. As an illustration of the various influences, the factors accounting for the change in the supply of money for a ten-year period ending in 1967 are indicated in Table III-4. From the end of 1957 to the end of 1967, the supply of money expanded from £198.6 million to £358.8 million, an increase of £160.2 million. Major factors contributing to an *expansion* included the increase in domestic credit (about £261 million) and the increase in net external assets (about £104 million). The major factor contributing to a *decline* in the supply of money was the accumulation of a 'near money'; deposit accounts increased to the extent of about £194 million.

A major function of a central bank is to effect changes in the supply of money in such a way as to achieve price stability and economic growth. The difficulty that the Irish Central Bank has in accomplishing this task relates to the fact that it has virtually no direct influence on changes in external assets. Furthermore, it has only recently acquired limited influence over credit conditions and other factors contributing to changes in the money supply. Irish commercial banks have traditionally been in a highly liquid position and the Central Bank for many years did not influence their credit policy. However, in 1965, the ratio of net external assets of commercial banks to their deposit liabilities dropped to an unusually low level (about 17 per cent). At that time, the commercial banks sought the advice of the Central Bank on the appropriate type of credit policy; it appears that since that time the Central Bank has attained a more important influence on credit and money essentially in an advisory capacity. Yet this influence is far from complete in part because certain factors which affect the net external assets of the banking system are beyond the control of the Central Bank.

1. The International Monetary Fund opposes the use of the freely fluctuating rate and equates it with an unstable rate. See International Monetary Fund. *Annual Report*. Washington: 1962, pp. 58-62.
2. Although the IMF's *International Financial Statistics* table on international liquidity includes only that foreign exchange held by central banks, governments and official entities, the separate country tables include as a sub-item under international liquidity the net external holdings of commercial banks. This would suggest that the IMF recognizes that such holdings could also be included as reserves.

CHAPTER IV

PAYMENTS ARRANGEMENTS: THE IMF AND THE STERLING AREA

The nature and conditions of the Irish foreign exchange market are based almost completely upon two institutional arrangements, the International Monetary Fund (IMF) and the Sterling Area. The Irish pound is a 'convertible' currency according to the IMF's definition of the term, but it is a convertibility which applies largely to Sterling Area transactions. Ireland has been a member of the Sterling Area from the time of its early informal beginning; she became a member of the IMF in 1957.

Conditions which prompted the establishment of the International Monetary Fund can be traced as far back as the 1930's. Chaos and uncertainty had characterized the foreign exchange markets; a contracting volume of international trade resulted from and also accentuated the spread of the depression throughout the world. 'Competitive depreciation' of exchange rates was employed by governments as an anti-depression measure in a vain effort to increase the level of exports and domestic employment. With the advent of World War II, comprehensive regulations and techniques to supplant the free market – bilateral agreements, state trading and exchange controls – were employed in an attempt to ensure an efficient use of resources for military and civilian needs. It was against this background that representatives of the major trading countries convened in 1944 to develop an international financial institution which could create order and freedom in the foreign exchange markets.

Purpose and nature of the IMF. Two financial institutions emerged from these conferences, the International Bank for Reconstruction and Development (examined in Chapter VII) and the IMF; both commenced operations in 1947. A major over-all objective of the IMF is to develop a multilateral payments system which is recognized as a prerequisite to a high level of world trade and investment. In the absence of a multilateral payments system, currencies cannot be freely exchanged for each other; if extensive inconvertibility exists, bilateral balancing of accounts between nations becomes necessary and severely restricts world commerce.

In order to achieve its objectives, the IMF was designed to promote stable rates of exchange, to provide an orderly means of altering unrealistic (under-valued or over-valued) rates of exchange, to induce member countries to abolish exchange controls, and to supply short-term loans to countries experiencing balance of payments difficulties. The basic objectives of the IMF have been widely accepted throughout the world economy (with the exception of most of the Communist Bloc countries which do not participate in the Fund). By mid-1968, over 100 countries participated as members; financial resources, the result of quotas allotted to member countries, amounted to the equivalent of about $21 billion. Ireland's initial quota was set at $30 million (£10.7 million); in accordance with a formula determining the composition of contributions, she contributed $4.5 million (£1.6 million) in gold and $25.5 million (£9.1 million) in Irish currency. Because of subsequent decisions to expand quotas, Ireland's contribution to the Fund amounts to the equivalent of $80 million.

The IMF functions on the premise that exchange rates which are stabilized within a narrow range induce certainty and confidence in world trade and investment. Freely floating rates are presumed to fluctuate widely, frequently and unpredictably and therefore to create uncertainty for traders and investors. Thus in the Articles of Agreement of the IMF member countries agree to peg the rate of exchange within a range of 1 per cent above and 1 per cent below the official rate. The official or par value of each currency, in turn, must be specified when a country first joins the Fund; it must be expressed in terms of either gold or the U.S. dollar. The par value of the Irish pound is 14.6 units per troy ounce of gold. Alternatively, one Irish pound equals $2.40.

The IMF and balance of payments disequilibrium. The Fund advocates stable exchange rates but it is recognized that structural changes in the world economy may render some rates of exchange unrealistic. Unequal rates of economic growth, the exhaustion or new discovery of natural resources, shifts in consumer demand, or a changing attitude toward world investment may affect the foreign exchange market in such a way as to contribute to the under- or over-valuation of certain currencies. Accordingly, the IMF makes provision for orderly rate adjustments in those instances where a country experiences persistent or fundamental rather than a transitory disequilibrium in its balance of payments. Generally the IMF sanctions changes in the official rate in those instances in which a country experiences chronic balance of payments disequilibrium involving a continuing loss in foreign exchange reserves that cannot be corrected by means other than severe domestic deflation or more restrictive import barriers. A country may initiate action to alter its rate by 10 per cent or less independently; if an adjustment in excess of 10 per cent is desired, the action must be approved by other members of the Fund.

Ireland has chosen to maintain her currency at a par with the British pound and has altered her rate of exchange concurrent with British devaluations. Until September of 1949, one pound equalled $4.03; in the following period and until November of 1967, one pound equalled $2.80. Since late 1967, it has equalled $2.40. The Irish decision to maintain a one-to-one ratio with sterling has been her own. As an independent country she is free to select any rate which is compatible with her best economic interests.

The IMF also provides a secondary source of foreign exchange reserves for countries experiencing balance of payments deficits of a transitory character. Exchange rates are stabilized or held within a narrow range of movement by member countries. It is not likely that in the short-run such rates will always equate the amount of foreign exchange demanded with the amount supplied as to a great extent these amounts reflect decisions made by private individuals and business firms dealing in world commerce. A country experiencing a deficit would tend to deplete its own foreign exchange reserves to hold the exchange rate within the specified range; in the absence of additional reserves from the Fund, the country might be forced to alter its rate of exchange or to pursue restrictive commercial policies almost immediately. To avoid unnecessary movements in the rate of exchange, the imposition of more restrictive trade barriers and quantitative controls, or depressive domestic policies adversely affecting employment in the deficit country, the IMF stands ready to supply it with the foreign currencies of which it is experiencing a shortage. Ireland, for example, after experiencing a balance of payments deficit in 1965, secured the equivalent of $22.5 million (about £8.0 million) in January of 1966.

Technically, IMF transactions are not loans, but rather are exchanges of currency with the deficit country exchanging its currency for those of which it is experiencing a shortage or which can be spent throughout the world. The amount a country can secure under its 'drawing rights' is generally limited to 25 per cent of it contributions to the Fund for each of a maximum of five years, but the 25 per cent annual limit is frequently waived. An amount equivalent to the *first* 25 per cent (called the 'gold tranche') is available almost automatically; for greater amounts the deficit country may be required to provide evidence that it is applying corrective measures, such as a policy to curb inflationary pressures, to alleviate the deficit. For the privilege of exercising its drawing rights, the deficit country pays a service charge which varies up to a maximum of 5 per cent of the amount borrowed; it must also make repayment (i.e., return the borrowed currency in exchange for its own) within three to five years or sooner if possible. The short-term nature of the loans is consistent with the concept of the Fund as a source of reserves for temporary disturbances, not for persistent disequilibrium.

The IMF, in 1952, instituted what are termed 'stand-by agreements' which allow a member country anticipating a need for financial assistance to arrange with the Fund in advance to obtain such assistance if and when the need actually arises. Thus a country can secure assistance more quickly than what would otherwise be the case and can plan and implement domestic programmes with the certainty that assistance is available when needed.

The Fund opposes the use of exchange controls especially on current account transactions since the practice is incompatible with a multilateral trade and payments system. However, the Fund condoned the use of existing controls during the early post-World War II period although they were to be withdrawn as soon as conditions permitted. Essentially, the abandonment of exchange controls by a country meant that the exchange rate would be determined largely by the forces of the free market with only occasional intervention on the part of a government agency operating a stabilization fund to keep the rate within the required range. Fund members are committed to assume eventually the obligations of Article VIII, Sections, 2, 3 and 4 of the Articles of Agreement; that is, they are to avoid the use of quantitative restrictions on current payments and the use of multiple exchange rates. Actually, it was not until 1958 that many countries felt their currencies could be placed on a convertible status. Less than one-third of the member countries had accepted the obligations of Article VIII, Sections 2, 3 and 4, by 1958, but the currencies of these countries represented about 80 per cent of the Fund's assets of this type and the countries were the source of 75 per cent of world exports.

Recent change in the I M F. The IMF has had an important influence on world monetary affairs. A number of modifications in its structure suggest that it is a viable institution capable of meeting and adapting to new conditions in the world economy. Modifications include the introduction of stand-by agreements; a willingness to waive certain requirements in order to provide badly-needed balance of payments assistance; the introduction of 'compensatory financing' which is particularly suited to 'one-crop', underdeveloped countries; and the expansion of quotas in 1959 and again in 1966. In addition, the IMF concluded an agreement, known as the General Agreement to Borrow, with ten of its major industrial member countries in 1962.[1] As a result, the Fund can readily mobilize additional financial resources to cope with serious

TABLE IV–1
EXCHANGE RESERVES OF IMF MEMBER COUNTRIES, 1958 AND 1967[a]

(billions of U.S. dollars)

Type of reserve	1958	1967
Gold	$38.0	$40.6
Reserve Position in the Fund	2.6	5.9
Foreign Exchange	17.0	25.7
Total	$57.6	$72.2

[a]Figures are for the end of 1958 and for the end of third quarter, 1967.

Source: International Monetary Fund. *International Financial Statistics* (March 1968). Washington: 1968, p. 16.

monetary conditions among the ten major industrial countries. The countries stand ready to lend their currencies (involving the equivalent of $6 billion) to the Fund to be made available, in turn, to one or more of the remaining ten participating countries which might be experiencing balance of payments difficulties. This Agreement is particularly useful in instances where heavy drawings have already been made on the Fund and it would otherwise lack a sufficient holding of convertible currencies to be of great value to deficit countries.

Special Drawing Rights. For several years there has been a concern among the major trading countries that the growth in world reserves has not been sufficient to accommodate an expanding volume of world trade and investment. As indicated in Table IV–1, the exchange assets of IMF countries increased about 25 per cent during the years 1958 through 1967.

The concern over reserve adequacy, coupled with developments in the world gold market, finally led to concrete proposals for a supplementary type of reserve (Special Drawing Rights) in 1967 and 1968. A major factor contributing to the adoption of the special reserves was the further possibility that the two major components of existing reserves (gold and foreign exchange) were not likely to increase in volume as greatly in future years.

As indicated in Table IV–1, much of the increase in world reserves has been the result of the growth of foreign exchange holdings; this reflects particularly the increased holdings of dollar and sterling claims against the United States and Great Britain on the part of other countries. As noted in Chapter III, it has been the balance of payments deficits of the United States and Great Britain in recent years which has enabled other countries to build up their holdings of foreign exchange. However, a new determination on the part of these two countries to terminate, or at least mitigate, the size of their deficits means that the significant growth of this type of world reserve is no longer to continue. Renewed efforts have been made to curb the U.S. deficit as an increased number of countries have become less willing to hold short-term dollar claims because of a fear of possible devaluation of the dollar.

The possibility of a devaluation of the dollar and a change in the price of gold led to speculation and chaotic conditions in the world gold market and finally contributed to the establishment of a two-price world gold market in early 1968. One price, a free-market price, reflects the demand and supply of buyers and sellers largely for industrial purposes and for private hoarding. The second price remains at $35.00 per ounce reflecting purchases and sales of monetary gold stocks, those stocks held by central banks and treasuries as backing for domestic money and as international reserves. Sales of monetary gold in the free market by official institutions of countries are presumably precluded as a result of a refusal on the part of the U.S. government to replenish the gold stocks of such countries.

In April of 1968, the finance ministers of the major industrial powers (with the exception of France) agreed to a plan for a new monetary reserve asset termed Special Drawing Rights (SDRs); if the plan is put into operation, additional liquidity would be created to supplement gold and convertible currencies. The proposed SDRs are essentially book entries of credit in a special drawing account of the IMF. They are denominated in terms of the gold equivalent of one U.S. dollar and allocated to members of the IMF in proportion to membership quotas. A country is entitled to use its SDRs if it is experiencing a balance of payments deficit. This is accomplished by transferring the SDRs to the account of those countries whose currencies are required by the deficit country. Receiving countries – presumably those experiencing balance of payments surpluses – are obligated to accept a specified amount of SDRs in exchange for their currency. The accumulated SDRs cannot be exchanged for gold; however, because they can be used for balance of payments purposes, they supplement gold and other exchange reserves and thus would represent an addition to world liquidity.

The approval of 60 per cent of the IMF member countries representing at least 80 per cent of the total voting power of the institution is required before the SDR plan will go into effect. All IMF countries are eligible to take advantage of the arrangement; however, individual countries may elect not to participate.

It would appear that the SDR system is essentially a formalized procedure whereby balance of payments deficit countries can acquire short-term credit from those countries whose currencies they are experiencing a shortage of. As a result, less reliance is placed on gold and reserve currencies as the basis for a growth in world liquidity. However, like most arrangements of this type, success of IMF operations depends upon the voluntary cooperation of member countries.

Ireland and the IMF. Ireland has borrowed from the IMF on but one occasion (early 1966); the amount was equivalent to $22.5 million. Part of the loan, $1.3 million, was repaid later in 1966. Ireland's $80 million subscription to the Fund amounted to $19.7 million in gold and the equivalent of $60.3 million in local currency. Accordingly, even with just one borrowing from the Fund, she was able to mobilize an amount of external reserves slightly in excess of her initial gold contribution. Under current provisions she could conceivably borrow as much as an additional $78.5 million in foreign exchange during the four succeeding years.

The advantages of the IMF to a foreign trade oriented economy such as Ireland's are obvious, but are sufficiently important to warrant some elaboration. In an economy heavily dependent on foreign trade, it is imperative that certainty and stability, as accommodated by the IMF, prevail in world commerce. Currency convertibility and multilateral trade are essential if Irish exporters are to sell in high-price markets and if importers are to buy in low-price markets.

Certain indirect benefits are also afforded to Ireland. This stems from the fact that the success and strength of the Irish economy are closely related to the viability of its trading partners. The General Agreement to Borrow, for example, directly benefits only the ten participating industrial countries. Yet these ten countries absorb virtually all of Irish exports and accordingly it is to Ireland's advantage if they can avoid prolonged balance of payments difficulties and thus remain willing to engage actively in world trade. U.S. efforts to improve its balance of payments position by discouraging the travel of Americans abroad, for example, has threatened the Irish tourist industry.

Ireland and the Sterling Area. It was noted in the previous chapter that Irish banks hold most of their foreign exchange reserves as sterling claims, that London banks are typically involved in Ireland's commercial transactions with the rest of the world, that the Irish pound is rigidly pegged to the British pound, and finally that capital moves freely between the two countries. Actually, these are the key characteristics of the exchange systems of all members of the Sterling Area with respect to Great Britain. Accordingly, these features apply to other member countries which include most of the Commonwealth countries (such as Australia, Ceylon, Cyprus, Gambia, Ghana, India, Kenya, Kuwait, Malasia, New Zealand, Nigeria, Pakistan, Singapore, South Africa and Zambia) as well as several non-Commonwealth countries (Burma, Iceland, Iraq, Jordan and Libya).

The Sterling Area developed in a gradual, unplanned fashion as Britain and other countries found it necessary to abandon the gold standard in the 1930's. During that period, Ireland and several other countries and territories having a close commercial relation with Britain linked their currencies to the pound sterling. For the Irish pound, the legal tie with sterling stems from a statutory obligation on the part of the Central Bank to redeem Irish legal tender notes in sterling at the Bank of England.

Although the character and the composition of the Sterling Area have changed over the years, it has continued to provide major advantages to the participating countries. The pound sterling, as both a reserve and a trading currency, has not only facilitated the trade and investment transactions of member countries, but has also induced confidence and stability in their monetary institutions. The overseas member countries hold deposits in London banks as well as other sterling claims as their reserves against domestic deposit liabilities and currency. The deposits serve as exchange reserves and also as working balances to accommodate the needs of private traders. Transactions of member countries with countries outside the Area involve the use of a sterling balance because it is a currency which is widely known and accepted. Within the Area itself there is full convertibility; for many of the member countries, this represents a large share of their total trade; transactions with countries outside the area have generally been restricted somewhat although this depends upon the regulations of the individual member country and the type of transaction to be undertaken.

Reserves held as sterling deposits are also used to the common advantage of member countries. If one or more of the member countries find their reserves approaching depletion as a result of a balance of payments deficit, they can secure reserves from other members which at the time are in a stronger position.

As holder of the reserve currency, Britain bears an additional burden in world trade and finance. However, there are some offsetting advantages accruing to Britain including the use of short-term funds on deposit in London and, because of the commercial ties among participating countries, ready access to the markets of member countries for her manufactured exports.

If sterling should be used to a lesser extent as an international reserve currency, or if the proportion of Ireland's trade with non-Sterling Area countries should rise, a much greater share of Ireland's external reserves is likely to take the form of dollar claims or short-term claims against the countries of the European Economic Community. Although the weight of tradition and the practical aspects of trade have favoured the use of sterling in the past, a gradual transition to the use of other currencies could be accomplished with little or no disruption of Ireland's commercial activity.

Irish exchange restrictions. Ireland has accepted the obligations of Article VIII, Sections 2, 3 and 4 of the Agreement of the International Monetary Fund and is expected to avoid the use of controls on current account payments or the imposition of multiple exchange rates. Subject to certain conditions, she is expected to stand ready to purchase balances of Irish pounds which might be held by foreigners.

Nevertheless, Ireland, as well as most other countries which have accepted the obligations of Article VIII, does employ controls over certain transactions. Ireland first used exchange controls in 1939. Great Britain at that time had entered the war and found it necessary to impose exchange controls to prevent a flight of capital from London and to facilitate control over exports and imports for war purposes. Ireland, as a member of the Sterling Area, found it necessary to introduce similar regulations. Exchange control operations came under the direction of the Minister for Finance who was given power to restrict payments abroad and to introduce other features of such a system. In 1950, Irish banks took over part of the exchange control operations; with the establishment in 1950 of the European Payments Union and its subsequent development, exchange restrictions were significantly relaxed by Ireland as well as by most European countries.

The controls imposed by Ireland over external payments are administered by the Central Bank although much of the authority for approving normal payments has been delegated to certain commercial banks. Because of Ireland's membership in the Sterling Area, payments to and from other parts of the Area are not subject to control and may be made freely in any Sterling Area currency, both for current and capital account transactions. Since by far the greatest share of Ireland's trade and capital movements is with other members of the Sterling Area most external transactions are conducted freely and outside the scope of exchange control authorities.

Transactions with countries outside the Sterling Area are treated as non-resident transactions and are subject to certain restrictions. These restrictions affect the value and type of export and import trade as well as the type of currency which can be used. Imports from outside the Sterling Area require prior approval (an import licence) under two circumstances: if the commodity is one of a limited range of commodities subject to quantitative restrictions or quotas, or if the item ordered from abroad is not to be delivered for at least nine months. All other imports of goods are free of import licensing. Payments for all invisibles (various types of services) outside the Area also require approval. Authorization to use either Irish pounds or sterling to finance authorized imports is granted automatically.

Exports to countries outside the Sterling Area also impose certain obligations upon the exporter. For large shipments (those with a value in excess of £100) payment must be received within six months. Proceeds for exports must be in the form of Irish pounds, Sterling or one of several specified convertible currencies; the latter must be sold by the exporter to an authorized bank for Irish pounds.

All transfers of capital to countries outside the Sterling Area require approval of the exchange control authorities. If the transfer is being made by a family planning to emigrate, an amount up to £5,000 is approved automatically. Applications for all other capital transfers to non-Sterling Area countries are considered on their merits. Generally there are no regulations imposed on capital *inflows* other than that the convertible currency received must be sold to an authorized bank. In addition, the purchase of unquoted securities and nonurban land requires prior approval.[2]

1. Member countries are Belgium, Canada, France, Germany, Italy, Japan, the Netherlands, Sweden, the United Kingdom and the United States.
2. For a summary of exchange restrictions employed by Ireland and other members of the International Monetary Fund, see International Monetary Fund. *Report on Exchange Restrictions* (Published annually), Washington, D.C.

CHAPTER V

EXTERNAL EQUILIBRIUM

Balance of payments equilibrium prevails for a country when, at the existing rate of exchange, autonomous payments equal autonomous receipts or when there is no long-term tendency for exchange *reserves* to rise or to fall. Under a system in which the exchange rate is not pegged or not controlled by the government, equilibrium exists when free market forces are such that there is no long-term tendency for the exchange *rate* to rise or fall. A variety of forces affecting the supply of and demand for foreign exchange may contribute to balance of payments disequilibrium. Some of the more important factors include: discovery or exhaustion of natural resources; political factors which affect the flow of commodity and investment movements; changes in consumer tastes and demands; uneven rates of growth in the world economy; technological advancements which reduce production costs; and inflationary pressures which lead to changes in the general price level.

When a country experiences balance of payments disequilibrium (either a deficit or a surplus), certain automatic adjustments occur through changes in income, prices or the rate of exchange to restore equilibrium. If the rate of exchange is stabilized or held constant through the use of exchange controls, internal movements in prices and income promote balance of payments equilibrium. In the absence of stabilization operations or a controlled exchange market, movements in the exchange rate serve to accommodate external equilibrium, although subsequent internal price and income changes are likely to occur.

In this chapter, key features of the balance of payments adjustment process with respect to exchange rates, incomes and prices will be briefly reviewed.[1] In the following chapter, attention will be directed toward recent theoretical modifications which show an interrelationship between the current and capital accounts and which, because of certain underlying assumptions, seem more descriptive of the 'open economy'.

Freely-fluctuating exchange rate. Under freely-fluctuating or flexible exchange rate systems, there is no 'par of exchange' because the value of the monetary unit is not defined in terms of precious metals or other currencies. Thus a change in either the demand for or the supply of foreign exchange is likely to lead to a movement in the rate of exchange which, in turn, is allowed to seek its own level. If the price of foreign exchange rises (falls), imports become more (less) expensive in terms of the domestic currency and exports become less (more) expensive in terms of the foreign currency. At the new rate of exchange, the amount of foreign exchange demanded and supplied is equated and balance of payments equilibrium prevails. Internal adjustments in prices and incomes are likely to follow, but on the whole, the brunt of the adjustment is borne by the exchange rates.

Whether a flexible exchange rate moves within a narrow margin or whether it is subject to violent fluctuations depends upon the price elasticities of foreign exchange supply and demand. A change in the demand for or supply of foreign exchange will lead to small movements in the rate of exchange if both are quite elastic (described in a later section). If demand and supply are relatively inelastic, substantial rate changes are needed to restore equilibrium. As noted later, elasticities of demand and supply are also important in determining the capacity of revaluation of a fixed exchange rate to correct balance of payments disequilibrium.

Despite the absence of an upper limit or a lower limit (except zero) to its fluctuations, and despite the absence of a mint par, the flexible exchange rate is believed to vary around a norm. This norm, known as the 'purchasing power parity rate,' is assumed to be an equilibrium rate which reflects relative price levels in the various trading countries. According to this theory, the rate of exchange adjusts itself to changes in internal price levels. It has also been suggested that the principle involved in the purchasing power parity theory should be used as a guide to the establishment of a new equilibrium exchange rate for those countries which stabilize the rate of exchange, but on occasion find either devaluation or appreciation necessary.

Devaluation and equilibrium. Since the end of World War II, most countries have fixed their exchange rates but have deliberately altered them when either persistent surpluses or deficits prevailed. Deficit disequilibrium has proved to require corrective action more frequently than surplus disequilibrium; accordingly, devaluation has been a more common occurrence than appreciation.

The technical or legal aspect of devaluation involves the redefinition of a currency in terms of gold and/or the U.S. dollar. For example, £1 initially equalled $2.80. With devaluation, the new par or official rate was set at £1 : $2.40.

But the important impact of devaluation is on the price, volume and the value of exports and imports. With devaluation, export prices are lowered in terms of foreign currencies thus providing a stimulus to exports; import prices rise in terms of local currency and as a result imports are discouraged. However, if devaluation is to improve a country's balance of payments position and thus give the country greater leeway in pursuing domestic policies, the foreign exchange *value* of exports must rise relative to the *value* of imports. This will occur if the relevant elasticities are favourable. If these elasticities are unfavourable which is not the usual situation, depreciation will worsen a country's balance of payments position. Devaluation is most likely to improve a country's balance of payments position if the domestic demand for imports is highly elastic and the foreign demand for exports is also elastic. This is even more certain to be true for the small country.

Consider first the impact of devaluation on the demand for imports. The price elasticity of demand for imports reflects the responsiveness of buyers to a movement in prices. If buyers are highly responsive to a change in the price of imports, demand is considered to be elastic over that price range. If buyers react only slightly, demand is considered to be inelastic. In more precise terms, if the percentage change in the quantity of imports demanded exceeds the percentage change in price, demand is elastic; if the percentage change in quantity demanded equals the percentage change in price, unitary elasticity prevails; and if the percentage change in quantity demanded is less than the percentage change in price, demand is inelastic.

When a country devalues, the price of imports will rise. Accordingly, the foreign exchange value of imports will decrease, but the value of imports will decrease most significantly the more elastic the demand for imports. Although the elasticity of demand for imports depends largely upon the types of commodities imported, a second major factor is the willingness of domestic firms to commence or expand production of competing or substitute items as prices become more favourable. Thus demand is most likely to be elastic if the domestic supply of competing or substitute items is elastic.

The elasticity of foreign demand for a country's exports is equally important in affecting the possibility of devaluation improving a country's balance of payments position. Devaluation lowers the foreign exchange price of exports and as a result the volume of exports is certain to increase. However, the foreign exchange value of exports can increase, decrease, or remain constant, if foreign demand is elastic, inelastic, or of unitary elasticity, respectively. Thus, for example, if the price of exports (in terms of the foreign currency) falls by 10 per cent, export earnings will rise only if the volume of exports increases by more than 10 per cent; if the volume of exports increases by less than 10 per cent, export earnings would actually fall.

The elasticity of foreign demand depends largely upon the foreign demand for various types of importable commodities. It also depends upon the elasticity of supply of substitute products in the importing countries.

In summary, devaluation lowers the price of a country's exports in terms of foreign currencies and raises the price of its imports in terms of the local currency. But whether or not devaluation improves the country's balance of payments position also depends upon the change in the volume of exports and imports. The greater the increase in the volume of exports and the decrease in the volume of imports, the more likely that the foreign exchange reserve position will be strengthened. The significance of the relevant elasticities is sometimes stated in terms of the 'Marshall-Lerner' condition as follows: devaluation will generally improve a country's balance of payments position if the sum of the coefficients of elasticities of demand for a country's exports and its demand for imports exceed one.

In November of 1967, deterioration in Great Britain's balance of payments position forced her to devalue the pound by 14.3 per cent. Although the Irish balance of payments was not in a weak position, it appeared to be in Ireland's interest to devalue simultaneously because of her close commercial ties with Britain. In addition, in view of Ireland's relatively high rate of unemployment, underemployment and emigration, it is possible that devaluation might give the government greater latitude in the use of monetary and fiscal policies insofar as it places her in an even stronger balance of payments and exchange reserve position.

Price changes and adjustment. When the rate of exchange is fixed, balance of payments adjustment occurs through changes in prices and income. Because movements in prices and income do not occur rapidly, exchange reserves are needed to finance short-run balance of payments disturbances.

Some of the early efforts to describe the balance of payments adjustment mechanism were based on the price-specie-flow theory. According to this theory movements in exchange reserves, the quantity of money, and the price level serve to restore balance of payments equilibrium.

As described in Chapter III, if a country's autonomous receipts exceed payments (a balance of payments surplus), that country's external reserves increase and the supply of money also rises. According to the price-specie-flow theory, the increase in the supply of money contributes to an increase in the price level. As inflation occurs, exports become more expensive and imports relatively less expensive. Accordingly, exports should decline, imports increase, and the balance of payments move from a surplus to an equilibrium position.

The process occurs in the opposite direction for a country experiencing a deficit. As noted in Chapter III, when autonomous receipts fall short of payments, external reserves and the supply of money both contract. According to the price-specie-flow theory, the decrease in the quantity of money leads to deflation; as a result exports become relatively less expensive and imports more expensive. Accordingly, the balance of payments will move from a deficit to an equilibrium position as exports rise and imports decline.

The domestic multiplier and income changes. Explanations which focus attention on the role of income changes to promote balance of payments equilibrium are derived from the domestic multiplier process. The domestic multiplier is used to describe the process by which a change in spending creates a multiple change in domestic income. It is usually assumed that the shift in spending is that which occurs with respect to real investment; consumption is assumed to be related directly to the level of income.

If, as an illustration, a firm increases its investment by expanding the size of its plant and equipment, an equivalent amount of new income is generated for workers, raw materials suppliers, professional persons and others directly affected by the investment decision. However, this is not the end of the process. Recipients of the income, in turn, spend part of their receipts for a variety of goods and services creating a new group of income recipients who also spend a share of their receipts for additional goods and services, and so on. Ultimately, the total income created is several times greater than the initial change in investment spending. The extent to which total income is generated depends upon the share of additional receipts actually spent (the marginal propensity to consume).

The portion of any additional income received which is saved or not spent for consumption is termed a 'leakage' as it represents a withdrawal of purchasing power from the income stream. If government transactions and external trade are assumed to be negligible, the total change in savings would ultimately increase until it equals the initial change in investment. At the new equilibrium, $S = I$, with S representing savings; I, investment.

Alternatively, a *decrease* in spending will lead to a multiple decline in income. With the initial fall in spending, some income recipients find that their earnings are smaller and they in turn spend less. The process continues until ultimately total income falls by some multiple of the initial drop in spending.

A key value in this process is that of the multiplier. The multiplier (k) is defined as:

$$k = \frac{1}{MPS}$$

with the MPS representing the marginal propensity to save. The extent to which a change in income occurs as a result of a change in investment (an injection) depends upon the value of the multiplier and that of the initial change in investment. That is:

$$dY = k \times dI$$

where dY represents a small change in income, and dI represents a small change in investment.

Assume for purposes of a numerical illustration that government transactions and foreign trade are negligible, that the MPS for an economy is 25 per cent, and that spending for investment rises by £1,000. In this 'first period', income received rises by £1,000. In the second period, £750 are spent (75 per cent of the receipts) generating an equivalent amount of income, and £250 are saved. In the third period, £562 are spent (75 per cent of £750) generating an equivalent amount of income; £187 are saved (25 per cent of £750). In the fourth period, £422 are spent for consumption and £141 are saved. As the process continues, the amounts spent and saved during each round grow smaller and smaller. But eventually the aggregate income created will total £4,000 (i.e., 4 × £1,000); the amount saved will equal £1,000 (i.e., 25 per cent of £4,000). Consumer spending would increase by £3,000.

The preceding analysis assumed the injection or stimulus to be a *single* increase in investment. The increased investment was followed by a higher level of income and savings. But as investment dropped back to the original level, income and savings would also decline to their original level. If, on the other hand, the volume of investment were to change permanently – a *sustained* injection – the volume of income, consumption, and savings would also move in a corresponding fashion to a new permanent level.

The implications of government action can be readily incorporated into the above analysis. Changes in government spending are comparable to changes in investment as both represent injections to cause a multiple change in income. Taxes, like savings, represent a leakage or a withdrawal from the income stream. The value of the multiplier in this case would equal 1/1 – the marginal propensity to consume (or 1/the marginal propensity to save plus what might be termed the marginal propensity to pay taxes). The equilibrium equation would be:

$$I + GS = S + T$$

with GS representing government spending; T, taxes.

The analysis also assumes that for real income to increase as a result of a higher level of investment, there must be unused domestic resources. Otherwise an expansion in domestic activity would largely reflect a price increase. Money income would increase, as described by the multiplier process, but real output would change little. In either case, however, the change in real income or prices would continue until equilibrium was restored.

The foreign trade multiplier. Explanations of the role played by changes in income in promoting balance of payments equilibrium employ the foreign trade multiplier concept. With the foreign trade multiplier, exports are assumed to be comparable to domestic investment because both are injections which affect domestic income in a similar fashion. Imports, a leakage, are comparable to savings; as income rises, imports rise and as income decreases, imports fall.

Assume as an illlustration that a country experiences a growth in the value of exports. Incomes will rise in the export sector and as recipients spend the proceeds, internal income is generated in the same way as with the domestic multiplier. In addition, the country's imports, which are a function of income, will also rise. In the absence of an increase in other leakages (savings and taxes) imports would expand until they equal the initial change in exports.

A decrease in exports will cause a decline in domestic income in the same fashion as a decrease in internal investment. The extent of the decline will depend upon the value of the multiplier which is determined by the marginal propensity to save and the marginal propensity to import (MPI).

Assume for purposes of a numerical example that for a given economy, government transactions are negligible, domestic savings remain constant, the MPI is 20 per cent, and exports increase by £1 million. The value of the multiplier ($k = 1/MPI$) is 5; accordingly, domestic income would ultimately increase by £5 million. Imports, the only leakage, would rise by £1 million, accordingly equalling the initial change in exports and thus restoring balance of payments equilibrium.

As a second illustration, assume the MPS $= 10$ per cent, the MPI $= 15$ per cent, and that exports rise by £10,000. The value of the multiplier would be 4, as $k = 1/MPS + MPI$. Accordingly, domestic income would rise by £40,000; savings by £4,000 and imports by £6,000. In this instance, it will be noted that the change in imports does not equal the initial change in exports and accordingly a current account surplus would exist. This would occur in any instance in which the MPS was a positive value greater than zero. Thus it would also be necessary to assume that a long-term capital outflow would accommodate or finance the difference so that over-all balance of payments equilibrium might exist. In this case, the equilibrium formula is:

$$I + EX = S + IM$$

where EX represents exports; IM represents imports.

It is again necessary to distinguish between a temporary change in exports (a single injection) and a permanent change in exports. With the former, domestic income and imports change temporarily and return to their original level. With the latter, income and imports shift but remain at the new level.

There is then a tendency for balance of payments equilibrium to be restored through movements in income. If a country experiences a current account surplus as a result of an increase in exports, domestic income will rise by a multiple amount; imports will also expand thus reducing or eliminating the current account surplus. If there is a current account deficit caused by a decrease in exports, domestic income will decline by a multiple amount; imports will also decrease and thus the deficit will be reduced or eliminated.[2]

Although balance of payments adjustments occur automatically, their impact may be at least partially modified by various types of government policies. This usually occurs when the adjustments in income and prices are such that one of the consequences is that of internal unemployment.

The foreign trade multiplier is also employed to explain the transmission of prosperity and recession from country to country. Thus an economy with an increase in autonomous domestic spending and income is likely to transmit the prosperity abroad as its imports rise. Other countries' exports will rise and through the multiplier process will experience a growth in their internal income. Similarly a recession resulting from a decrease in domestic spending will create a current account surplus for that country as imports decline. But the corresponding fall in other countries' exports is likely to depress their internal incomes.

Price versus income adjustments. The early theories pertaining to balance of payments adjustments emphasized the role of price changes; the more recent theories attach greater importance to the role of income changes. In principle, there is evidence that income changes may be more important in restoring balance of payments equilibrium for the small, open economy than are price changes.[3]

In order that the price mechanism be relevant, it is necessary to assume that relative price changes cause domestic buyers to switch from domestic- to foreign-produced goods and services in event of a balance of payments surplus, and from foreign- to domestic-produced goods in event of a deficit. But the ability to substitute in either direction assumes the productive capacity of the domestic economy is sufficiently flexible or possesses the capacity to transform to satisfy the changing demand requirements.

The small economy, however, does not possess a 'rounded' productive structure; it lacks the size and diversity of resources to produce a wide range of consumer and producer goods. Accordingly, there is a low degree of substitutability between imports and domestic production.

The more 'modern' explanations relate exports and imports to income rather than to prices. Thus a rise in exports would lead to greater imports as income increased. The additional imports, however, would be the result of a higher level of income rather than a shift in prices. Such imports would reflect a higher level of domestic consumption of goods and services, rather than being a substitute for domestic items. Similarly, a fall in exports would lead to contracted imports as domestic incomes declined. But the decline in imports would reflect a shrinkage of domestic consumption, rather than a switch toward domestic goods and services.

In principle, it would appear that income changes would be more important in affecting balance of payments equilibrium for Ireland than would price changes. Ireland is not only an unusually open economy, but also the elasticity of substitution between domestic and foreign goods is small. Ireland's imports to a great extent represent raw materials, capital goods, and certain finished consumer goods which cannot be readily produced internally.

1. For a comprehensive treatment of the adjustment process, see, for example, Charles P. Kindleberger. *International Economics*. Homewood, Illinois: Richard D. Irwin, Inc., 1963, pp. 63-214.
2. For the sake of simplicity, foreign repercussions of the multiplier are omitted. For the relatively small economy, such repercussions represent a negligible amount.
3. For a more complete analysis see Henry C. Wallich. *Monetary Problems of an Export Economy*. Cambridge, Mass.: Harvard University Press, 1950, pp. 212-216.

CHAPTER VI

DEVELOPMENTS IN IRELAND'S BALANCE
OF PAYMENTS

The balance of payments adjustment mechanisms described in the preceding chapter are most applicable to closed economies in which major disturbances are based on internal factors. In recent years, efforts have been made to identify other relationships and adjustment factors for the open economies. For analytical purposes, the term open economy has been applied either to regions within a larger political unit, or to entire countries heavily dependent upon world commerce. Two unique factors characterize the open economies: exogenous disturbances (changes in exports) are as important as internal ones; and factors of production are relatively mobile across their boundaries.

The purpose of this chapter is to analyze the characteristics of Ireland's balance of payments and domestic activity for the period 1950-1966. An effort will be made to identify a relationship between such aggregates as employment, national income, exports, capital formation, imports and capital inflows. Ireland, as noted earlier, is definitely an open economy with respect to external trade, capital and labour movements.

Domestic prosperity, investment and exports. A sufficient amount of data is available on an annual basis to trace in a general way the interrelationship of Ireland's domestic economy and commerce with the rest of the world. The relevant information for such an analysis for the years 1950 through 1966 is presented in Table VI–1. As a basis for the analysis, the status of the economy with respect to the level of domestic economic activity must be determined. The identification of three fairly distinct sub-periods of either relative prosperity or stagnation is possible on the basis of certain key indicators – the unemployment rate, the volume of output in the transportable goods industry, and values for both real and market GNP.

I 1950 through 1954 or 1955: relative prosperity as both real and market GNP and real output in the transportable goods industry increased;[1]

II 1955 through 1958 or 1959: relative stagnation as real GNP remained almost constant and unemployment was generally relatively high. Output in the transportable goods industry remained constant during the period 1955 through 1958, but increased in 1959. (Although not indicated in the data, the highest

TABLE VI–1
INDICATORS OF IRELAND'S ECONOMIC ACTIVITY
AND FOREIGN TRADE, 1950–1966

Year	Unemployment rate	Transport goods industry [a]	GNP [b] Mkt.	GNP [b] Real	Merch. exports	Dom. cap'l form.	Priv. cap'l. inflow	Current acc't. pos'n. [c]	Balance o/d paym'ts. pos'n. [d]
1950		91	£ 399	£562	£ 70	£ 57	£13	£—30	£ 4
1951	3.6%	94	421	573	80	72	19	—62	—38
1952	4.7	92	478	586	99	65	13	— 9	5
1953	5.3	100	519	601	112	80	19	— 7	14
1954	5.3	103	517	607	112	85	9	— 6	4
1955	5.1	108	540	607	107	91	— 8	—35	—47
1956	5.3	105	549	598	104	90	2	—14	—15
1957	6.7	104	569	601	127	79	1	9	7
1958	6.4	106	588	588	127	80	18	— 1	16
1959	6.1	118	624	614	127	83	15	— 9	4
1960	5.6	126	661	648	148	90	2	— 1	0
1961	5.0	137	710	679	170	108	14	1	14
1962	5.0	146	765	700	169	128	24	—13	10
1963	5.2	154	817	731	192	148	27	—22	3
1964	5.2	165	947	761	217	172	38	—31	5
1965	5.2	171	1001	780	215	193	25	—42	—18
1966	5.8	178	1045	786	235	191	50	—16	30

aFigures for the transportable goods industry represent a volume index
   with a base year 1953.
bFigures for real GNP are in 1958 prices.
cNegative figures indicate a current account deficit.
dNegative figures indicate a balance of payments deficit.

Source: Central Statistics Office, *Statistical Abstract* (Annual). Dublin,
       Stationery Office. Central Bank, *Report of the Central Bank*
       (Annual). Dublin. National Industrial Economic Council,
       Report on Full Employment. Dublin, Stationery Office, 1967.

rates of emigration during the entire period under study were for
the years 1954, 1955, 1956, 1957, 1959 and 1960. In general, these
years correspond with domestic stagnation.)

III 1959 through 1966: relative prosperity as both real and
market GNP and activity in the transportable goods industry rose,
and unemployment declined during most of the period. However,
the growth in economic activity leveled off in late 1965 and 1966.

As would be expected, the 'turning point' years, 1955 and 1959,
present a mixed picture and cannot be easily categorized in terms

of movements of the four indicators. Accordingly, these years can be identified only in an arbitrary fashion.

Assuming the three sub-periods are identified realistically, they can in turn be characterized with respect to domestic capital formation, exports, and the balance of payments position.

I 1950 through 1954 or 1955: relative prosperity. Exports and domestic investment expanding. A net 'private' capital inflow ranging from £9 million to £19 million if 1955 is excluded.[2] A current account deficit ranging from £6 million to £62 million.

II 1955 through 1958 or 1959: relative stagnation. Exports fell initially but increased slightly; domestic investment dropped but did not recover until 1960. Net capital inflow was small during 1956 and 1957, following an outflow which occurred during 1955; by 1958 and 1959, the capital inflow had recovered. The current account deficit was generally relatively small and a surplus prevailed during 1957.

III 1959 through 1966: relative prosperity. Exports and domestic investment increased at a high rate. A net private capital inflow from 1960 forward averaging about £25 million per year. A relatively large current account deficit (ranging from £13 million to 42 million) during each year from 1962 to 1966.

It is apparent that there is a relationship between the level of domestic activity, exports, domestic investment and capital inflows. However, the results of an empirical investigation involving the use of time series must be interpreted in a cautious fashion. The statistical techniques which are most appropriate cannot be readily determined in an objective fashion. In addition, the time lags which might be relevant for various response mechanisms cannot be identified from annual data. Finally, there are sharp fluctuations in private capital movements and in the current account deficit which are difficult to relate to other annual data.

It is apparent from Table VI–1 that there is an upward trend in the series representing GNP, exports and capital formation. The trend for each of the series can be expressed in an equation of the type:

$$Y = a + bX$$

with X the time period (the independent variable) and Y (the dependent variable) the trend value for period X. With a linear trend, periods of prosperity and stagnation are revealed.

Using a least squares method for obtaining a linear trend and data derived from Table VI–1 for the three series, the following estimating equations are obtained:

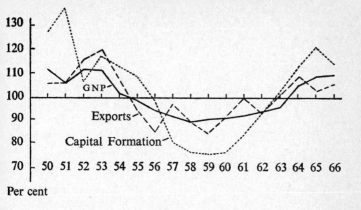

CHART VI-1a
ACTUAL VALUES OF GNP, EXPORTS AND CAPITAL
FORMATION AS PERCENTAGE OF TREND,
1950–1966

GNP

Exports

Capital Formation

Per cent

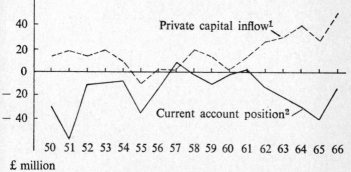

CHART VI-1b
PRIVATE CAPITAL INFLOW AND CURRENT
ACCOUNT POSITION,
1950–1966

Private capital inflow[1]

Current account position[2]

£ million

[1]Negative value reflects capital outflow
[2]Negative value reflects current account surplus

(i) GNP: $Y = 655.9 + 37.5\,X$
(ii) Domestic capital formation: $Y = 106.6 + 7.7\,X$
(iii) Merchandise exports: $Y = 141.8 + 9.5\,X$

81

In each case, the origin is 1958, and X units equal one year.

A comparison of the three series is of greater interest when the actual data for each are expressed as a percentage of the trend for that series. The results of such computations are reflected in Chart VI–1a. As would be expected, the three percentage-of-trend series follow a similar pattern. The values in each are generally below the trend during the years identified as those of stagnation (1955-1959) and above trend during most of the remaining prosperous years.

A significant degree of correlation is suggested by comparing the percentage-of-trend figures for GNP and each of the two remaining series.[3] The close correlation suggests a close association between GNP and each of the two 'injections'. Which of the two injections is most important as a causal factor cannot be readily established. Changes in domestic capital formation appear to lag behind major changes in export values. However, changes in GNP are more apparent when the *combined* values of exports and capital formation shift significantly.[4]

Capital movements and the current account position. One of the interesting features of Ireland's balance of payments position is that during the years when merchandise exports (a balance of payments receipt) were relatively high, the current account deficit (payments in excess of receipts) was also relatively large. That is, as indicated in Charts VI–1a and 1b, during most of the years when the value of actual exports was less then the long-term trend, the current account deficit was smaller than average; in many of the years when the value of actual exports exceeded the long-term trend, the current account deficit was larger than average.

This situation does not appear to correspond with conventional multiplier theory which assumes that a relatively high level of exports will occur along with a current account *surplus*. Nor can the large capital inflow which has coincided with domestic prosperity be readily explained with conventional theory which assumes a cause and effect relationship in either direction in the current and capital accounts. A plausible explanation for the developments in Ireland's balance of payments situation is a 'common cause' theory of adjustment – a synthesis of earlier views – presented by Professor Marina von Neumann Whitman.[5]

According to the common cause theory:

a) increases in domestic investment and in exports are not independent disturbances in the open economy; instead, the two are the result of some 'common cause' and thus are likely to be positively correlated;

b) an increase (decrease) in investment in the export sector is likely to be matched by a capital inflow (outflow);

c) thus an increase (decrease) in exports is likely to be matched by a capital inflow (outflow);

d) accordingly, export-led domestic prosperity may exist along with an external deficit, and a recession along with a surplus.

The common cause theory assumes changes in the balance of payments current and capital accounts to be the result of a shift in the anticipated rate of return (i.e., the common cause) in the export industries. Assume then an increase in the marginal efficiency of capital (MEC) in the export sector; exports as well as domestic investment will rise, and there may be initially a current account surplus. But with the higher MEC a capital inflow will occur (either simultaneously, shortly thereafter, or possibly even before); imports will also rise sharply as a result of increased domestic consumption and investment; because of a high propensity to import, this is likely to lead to a current account deficit.

Thus it is possible and even likely that expanding exports and investment in the export sector, while providing the stimulus for domestic growth, may occur along with a current account deficit as capital inflows occur and as imports rise to supply the requirements of domestic consumption and investment. In the *multiplier* theory, *export-led* prosperity and a current account deficit were not likely to occur simultaneously.

If, on the other hand, a domestic recession occurs as a result of a fall in the MEC in the export sector, according to the common cause theory, exports will decrease and contribute to a current account deficit. However, the fall in exports may be more than offset by a reduction in imports and a concurrent capital outflow. As a result, a current account surplus may prevail.

Thus a tentative pattern emerges in the interrelationship of developments with respect to Ireland's exports, imports, and capital formation if the mobility of capital across national boundaries is recognized as an integral part of the process. A rise in the MEC in the export sector involves a higher level of exports and capital inflows. Due to an accelerator type link, imports of capital goods increase; exports also have a high import content hence raw material imports rise; and, finally with domestic prosperity, consumer goods imports rise. The capital inflow facilitates imports; when combined with a high propensity to import for a rapidly growing open economy, current account deficits can be expected. The analysis underscores the importance of a dynamic export sector for the maintenance of a high level of exchange receipts – as a result of the actual export of goods and services, and as a result of capital inflows. Whether or not a large volume of exchange receipts through capital inflows is appropriate for Ireland in view of the subsequent obligation to service the debt will be considered in the following chapter. The capital inflow serves to supplement domestic savings, but also results in a claim against future foreign exchange earnings.

Stability of domestic income and production. One of the implications of the common cause formulation is that with export-led prosperity, foreign exchange receipts will rise sharply as both exports and the capital inflow increase. With recession, exchange receipts will fall sharply as exports and the capital inflow decline (or as a capital outflow occurs). Actually, certain institutional arrangements and other features of open economies, including Ireland's, mitigate the severity of fluctuations in income, employment and prices as part of the adjustment process. These factors are related to the propensity to import, and, for Ireland, commercial bank holdings of external assets.

Because of its narrow resource base and accordingly a low elasticity of supply, Ireland has a high propensity to import with respect to many types of consumer and investment goods. This is particularly true of certain types of raw materials and investment goods which are not available or cannot be produced readily in Ireland. One result of the high propensity to import is that domestic income, when affected by an exogenous influence, tends to be more stable than what would otherwise be the case. The larger the propensity to import, the smaller the change in domestic income that is required, following a change in exports, in order that imports move sufficiently to restore equilibrium.

A second factor is that Irish commercial banks hold a large share of their reserves against domestic liabilities in the form of external assets or sterling claims. Such external reserve holdings may serve to cushion the impact of short-run balance of payments disturbances on the domestic sector. That is, as balance of payments receipts exceed payments, external reserves of commercial banks increase. The external reserves fall as commercial banks expand domestic credit and as they acquire currency from the Central Bank to meet the needs of customers. But in practice, commercial banks do not always expand credit to the full extent possible. This is in part because the holdings of external assets provide an interest return and thus serve as an alternative to the extension of domestic credit. Alternatively if balance of payments receipts fall short of payments, the commercial banks might have to contract domestic credit in order to borrow external reserves from the Central Bank. But the fact that they can draw on the external investments to satisfy the needs of private traders in event of a balance of payments deficit means that they do not always find it necessary to borrow external reserves from the Central Bank. Accordingly, because the commercial banks can increase their holdings of external assets with a balance of payments surplus and contract them with a balance of payments deficit means that sharp changes in domestic credit and money are greatly modified. In other words, a gain in commercial bank external reserves when over-all receipts are expanding, or a fall in commercial bank external assets when receipts are not rising or falling, serves to neutralize the monetary impact of external disturbances.

Exchange rate stability and internal adjustments. Member countries of the International Monetary Fund have accepted the use of the fixed rate of exchange as a condition for stability and certainty in world commerce. Flexible or variable exchange rates are generally assumed to be unstable rates and accordingly inimical to interests of world trade and investment. As noted previously, with a flexible exchange rate system, a change in either the demand for or the supply of foreign exchange results in a new rate of exchange and balance of payments equilibrium prevails. The brunt of the adjustment is borne by the exchange rate although some change in incomes and prices follows.

If, on the other hand, the rate of exchange is fixed, balance of payments adjustments occur, not through changes in the rate of exchange, but through movements in prices and incomes. With stabilization funds, if the autonomous demand for foreign exchange exceeds the amount supplied at the given rate of exchange, exchange reserves of the banking system will decline and stabilization operations will be conducted. A limited amount of reserves may be secured from abroad, but if this proves insufficient, a fundamental disequilibrium exists and the country must alter the rate of exchange (normally a devaluation), impose exchange controls, or pursue a restrictive monetary policy. If devaluation or exchange controls are inappropriate for one of several reasons, automatic internal adjustments to prices and incomes must be reinforced with monetary and fiscal policy to accommodate balance of payments equilibrium. In other words, prices and incomes bear the brunt of the adjustments and must change to facilitate restoration of balance of payments equilibrium.

Thus in order to avoid a complete depletion of reserves, monetary and fiscal authorities must reinforce the adjustment process with policies which promote exports and discourage imports. As implied by the multiplier and common cause formulations, this might include a stringent monetary policy designed to discourage consumer spending and to avoid price increases. Fiscal policy might be employed to achieve similar objectives. If aggregate spending is reduced and price levels held in check, exports are likely to rise relative to imports and the balance of payments problem brought under control.

Deflationary policies of this type can be readily administered if the economy is experiencing full or over-full employment and inflationary pressures prevail. If, on the other hand, a high rate of unemployment exists or if there is a desire to encourage investment and promote economic growth, a conflict arises. Deflationary policies are likely to increase unemployment and discourage investment.

Over-all balance of payments position. Ireland maintains a fixed exchange rate and holdings of exchange reserves serve to even out differences between balance of payments credits and debits. When recognized that transactions in the current account and private capital account are largely free-market or unrestricted transactions, it is apparent why the external reserve position of the banking system must be watched closely.

During the seventeen-year period under consideration, Ireland experienced a balance of payments deficit – a decline in external reserves – during only four years. However, in those four years when a deficit did occur (1951, 1955, 1956 and 1965), its magnitude was relatively large and in the aggregate roughly equalled the aggregate surpluses of the remaining thirteen years. These deficits occurred when there was a large current account deficit. However, a large current account deficit did not always correspond with an over-all deficit; frequently, capital inflows were sufficient to offset the current account deficit and as a result foreign exchange reserves increased.

As noted previously, a high marginal propensity to import means that domestic income will fluctuate less as a *result* of external disturbances; however, at the same time, the government has less autonomy in the promotion of internal expansion because of a possible adverse effect on the over-all balance of payments. Thus a program of increased government spending to reduce unemployment is likely to lead to an increased volume of consumer and capital goods imports and, unless there is an increase in exports or capital inflows, a balance of payments deficit. Or a general wage increase in excess of productivity may cause a deterioration in the balance of payments situation because of a high propensity to import consumer and other goods.

A program of increased investment sufficient to promote economic growth and to reduce the flow of emigration encounters similar obstacles. Productive investment in the domestic sector makes the economy more efficient and able to compete in world markets in the long-run; but in the short-run it leads to increased imports of raw materials, capital goods and consumer products and possibly a balance of payments deficit. Thus domestic expansion to a great extent depends upon the continued availability of foreign exchange receipts from either exports or capital inflows.

The difficulty which Ireland has with a fixed exchange rate and limited foreign exchange reserves can be illustrated with a description of the 1965 situation. During that year the current account deficit amounted to £42 million and was only partially offset by the £25 million private capital inflow. As a result, exchange reserves declined sharply by £18 million (from £242 million at the beginning of the year to £224 million at the end of the year). When it became apparent in mid-1965 that the balance of payments situation was deteriorating, the government instituted measures to restrict demand despite an unemployment rate in excess of 5 per cent and emigration occurring at about 16,000 per year. This included a request by the Central Bank to commercial banks to reduce the growth in their lending operations and to discriminate in favour of loans for productive purposes; in addition, the public capital programme was curtailed somewhat. Price controls were also introduced in October of 1965. Finally, in early 1966, the Government obtained an £8.0 million loan from the IMF to strengthen its foreign exchange position.

The restrictive measures did help the balance of payments situation and external reserves continued to increase through the end of 1966. But the performance of the domestic economy, at least partially the result of restrictive monetary and fiscal action, was considerably poorer than in earlier years. Real GNP increased by only about 2.5 per cent in 1965 as compared with an average annual rate of nearly 4.5 per cent for the period 1958 through 1964. Output in the transportable goods sector increased at about half the rate in 1965 as in 1964. Even into 1966, the performance of the economy was moderate although it appeared to be improving significantly by 1967.

1. The relative prosperity of the period 1950-1955 (as well as the period 1960-1966) existed in the sense that the growth rate was higher than during the preceding years and during the years 1955-1959. Generally, Ireland's growth rate was considerably lower than that of other European countries during the three periods.
2. It is assumed that the behaviour of the 'private' capital movements is most relevant to this analysis. Accordingly, values for private capital flows exclude Irish government and bank borrowing and lending insofar as they can be readily identified. For some years, the value of

certain types of government borrowing cannot be determined and accordingly were not excluded.

3. The coefficient of correlation between the percentage-of-trend series for GNP and exports is $+.852$; the coefficient for GNP and domestic capital formation is $+.889$. These will be recognized as correlations of time series with the trend eliminated.

4. In a study by Leser, the Irish situation is pictured as one in which there are large autonomous changes in domestic consumption and investment, but the total of these gradually adjusts to the level of exports. See C. E. V. Leser. *A Study of Imports*. Dublin: The Economic and Social Research Institute. April 1967, p. 19.

5. Marina von Neumann Whitman. 'International and Interregional Payments Adjustment: A Synthetic View,' *Princeton Studies in International Finance*. Princeton, N. J.: Princeton University Press, 1967.

CHAPTER VII

CAPITAL MOVEMENTS

An important type of transaction in international commerce is the flow of short- and long-term capital or investment. Short-term movements, which were examined in Chapters II and III, are usually defined to include transactions involving currency, bank deposits, treasury bills and similar financial assets which mature in less than one year. Long-term capital movements, analyzed in greater detail in this chapter, are defined to include assets with an indefinite maturity or a maturity in excess of one year. Such a distinction is arbitrary at best and in practice the actual maturity date of an asset may not be a meaningful factor. Nevertheless the distinction between short- and long-term capital is useful for analytical purposes.

Nature of long-term capital movements. When a country experiences a capital outflow, the transactions are entered as debits or payments on its balance of payments. If a country is experiencing a *net* capital outflow or is running a deficit on its long-term capital account, its domestic residents (individuals, firms and governments) are investing in or buying the stocks and bonds of foreign countries, or foreigners are reducing their holdings of stocks and bonds in the first country. Assuming net short-term capital movements are negligible, such a country will be running a surplus of equal size on its current account; as an international lender, its exports of goods and services will exceed imports of goods and services. The current account surplus reflects the actual nature of capital outflows – a real transfer of goods and services from the lending to the borrowing country which accompanies the financial transfer in the capital accounts.

When a country experiences a capital inflow, transactions are entered as credits or receipts on its balance of payments. Such a country is an international borrower. Again, two general types of transactions are possible: foreigners purchase bonds and stocks of the borrower country, or domestic residents reduce their holdings of foreign stocks and bonds. In either case the net inflow permits the country to experience or to accomplish certain related situations or conditions: to run a deficit on its current account without necessarily experiencing an over-all balance of payments deficit; to maintain a level of domestic investment which exceeds current domestic savings; and to use internally an amount of goods and services which exceeds domestic production. Essentially, the major advantage of the capital inflow is to provide the borrowing country with access to external resources.

The greatest share of international investment over the years has been undertaken by private individuals and business firms in response to interest rate differentials and profit opportunities. However, since the end of World War II, a large share of investment capital has been provided by governmental or international agencies. Funds provided from these sources, especially from national governments, are less likely to be directly related to the anticipated monetary return; instead, they may be designed to promote reconstruction or development or even for political purposes in the borrowing country.

Advantages and disadvantages of capital movements. The advantages of a capital inflow are numerous: it provides the country with an additional volume and type of resources with which to expand productive capacity; it increases the marginal output and may facilitate the full utilization of complementary factors of production already within the country; it is frequently accompanied by managerial talent and technology; it expands the income and property base against which internal taxes can be levied; it frequently contributes to the expansion of productive capacity in new fields and industries.

As far as the borrowing country is concerned, a capital inflow not only represents a source of savings to be utilized, but also provides access to external raw materials, capital equipment or other items which may be difficult or impossible to produce domestically. In other words, for an economy attempting to expand productive capacity, there may be a shortage of savings and also a shortage of foreign exchange. Even if domestic savings could be expanded to permit additional investment, this may not lead directly to the additional foreign exchange needed for the specialized types of imports required for certain kinds of domestic investment. Capital inflows, on the other hand, may be utilized to solve both the savings and the foreign exchange problem.

From the economy's point of view, there are certain possible disadvantages associated with capital inflows. The major disadvantage is that of servicing the debt (interest, dividends and amortization) which requires the use of foreign exchange or, more basically, a net outflow of real resources from the debtor to the creditor country (or to any country with a convertible currency). A second possible disadvantage is that direct investment from abroad (i.e., the purchase by foreigners of common stocks or other securities with voting rights) represents a transfer of partial or complete control of a firm to non-residents. Under some circumstances, foreign owners may not act in a way consistent with the interests of the host country. This might occur, for example, if the investor withdraws a large volume of capital abruptly or at a time when the host country is experiencing balance of payments problems. Actually, some of these factors, such as an abrupt withdrawal of capital, can be controlled and prevented by the host country. But in general there is little reason to believe that the long-run profit interests of the foreign owner are incompatible with the economic objectives of the host country.

Ireland has experienced a current account deficit and capital account surplus during most years since the end of World War II. Since the beginning of 1947 and through the end of 1966 this amount has averaged about £17 million a year. The net borrower status is not unusual for an economy such as Ireland's in which extensive efforts are being made to industrialize; new investment from abroad greatly facilitates the process in that it provides capital goods and equipment, raw materials, managerial skills and other ingredients essential for industrialization. Perhaps the unusual characteristic of the Irish experience is the great extent to which domestic residents have invested abroad in the past. There is, of course, the possibility that a large and continuing current account deficit eventually contributes to balance of payments problems. The importance of capital inflows for the growth of the Irish economy is recognized by the Central Bank, among other official institutions. Yet there is a concern that too much reliance be placed on external capital and not enough on domestic savings. The concern is that external capital introduces a potentially unstable element into the economy should the inflow be reduced or existing capital be withdrawn as a result of external factors.[1]

A significant share of Ireland's capital account surplus since the end of World War II is the result of foreign disinvestment. This liquidation of past savings which were invested in foreign securities may be either advantageous or disadvantageous as far as Ireland's growth is concerned, depending upon a number of factors. If the foreign exchange acquired from the liquidation is employed to facilitate a productive type of domestic investment, rather than simply used to accommodate increased personal consumer expenditures, then the action may provide positive benefits to the economy. The major disadvantage is that once foreign stocks and bonds have been liquidated, they no longer provide a continuing source of foreign exchange receipts through the repatriation of profits and interest. Thus foreign disinvestment may be detrimental if it occurs as a substitute for domestic savings; in addition the possible balance of payments impact may be particularly adverse since once such assets are liquidated, the inflow of profits and interest also comes to an end.

In a sense, the effective impact of liquidating external assets on a country's over-all balance of payments position is not significantly different from the acquisition of new obligations to foreigners. In one case a source of foreign exchange earnings is lost; in the other, a new claim arises against foreign exchange earnings. In either case, the ultimate impact on a country's external position depends largely upon how effectively the proceeds of the capital movement are employed.

Servicing long-term capital obligations. Despite the advantage of capital inflows, it is also conceivable that a borrowing country may accumulate such a large externally-held debt that the servicing of the obligation (payment of interest, dividends, and repayment of principal) contributes to a balance of payments strain.

Since external debt servicing (a balance of payments debit or payment) requires the use of foreign exchange, the avoidance of a balance of payments problem depends upon the debtor country's capacity to earn or otherwise acquire foreign exchange. Debt servicing becomes a fixed obligation which must be met irrespective of other developments in the domestic economy and foreign trade sector.

All other things remaining equal, a country borrowing from abroad is least likely to experience difficulties servicing the debt when (i) the initial investment inflow is employed in productive projects which are either foreign-exchange earning (expansion of exports) or foreign-exchange saving (reduction of imports); (ii) the rate of return – interest or profits – is relatively low; (iii) the initial grace period and the total repayment period are relatively long; (iv) the exchange reserves held by the debtor country are relatively large; (v) the tariff policy of the creditor country is relatively liberal;[2] and (vi) the debtor country's exchange earnings are relatively stable over time.

It is apparent that many factors affect an economy's debt servicing capacity and that there is no precise formula for determining a 'safe' level of obligations. Occasionally, however, a measure of a country's position is used which is termed the 'external debt ratio':

$$\frac{\text{debt service (interest, dividends and amortization)}}{\text{foreign exchange earnings on current account}}$$

All other things remaining equal, the higher the ratio, the more likely the debtor country is to encounter balance of payments difficulties because a greater share of its exchange earnings on current account must be directed toward the fixed obligation involved in servicing debts held by foreigners. The external debt ratio may have some value for comparative purposes for a given country over a period of time. Generally, however, a more comprehensive analysis is needed to determine if a country is over-extending itself in terms of debt service obligations.

A somewhat more comprehensive technique for assessing the possibility of a future balance of payments crisis due to servicing external debt obligations is provided by Jan de Weille.[3] Essentially, this technique involves estimating, on the basis of past experience, the future value of certain major balance of payments components. The components estimated for a two to three year period are exports, imports, debt servicing, capital inflows, and gold and foreign exchange reserves.

Estimated export values, reflecting a linear extrapolation of trend values, are adjusted by being set at the minimum level reasonably possible reflecting past fluctuations in such values. Import values are estimated in a similar way with the deviation from past trends used as a measure of compressibility. Debt servicing is defined to include only that applicable to public or public-guaranteed debt. It is also assumed that all official reserves (official gold and foreign exchange reserves, and IMF drawing rights) are available for use.

After these values have been established, a country's anticipated 'net foreign exchange position' can be computed. It is defined as:

Gross capital inflow
plus Initial gold and foreign exchange reserves
less Import surplus (imports minus exports)
less Debt service.

A positive net foreign exchange reserve position implies that debt servicing can be readily continued along with the import surplus. A negative figure implies an impending balance of payments crisis. As is recognized by de Weille, this approach to assessing the vulnerability of a country's balance of payments to short-run fluctuations would have to be modified to take into consideration the particular characteristics of the country in question.

If sufficient statistical information were available to assess the vulnerability of Ireland's external position, two major modifications would have to be made. First, debt servicing would have to be redefined to include amortization and interest on non-guaranteed private debt and dividend payments on direct investment, as well as the servicing of public and public-guaranteed debt. The share of

Ireland's non-guaranteed private external debt is sufficiently large to require that it be included for a meaningful estimate of the economy's position. Second, it would be necessary to recognize that not all of Ireland's reserves are available in event of a crisis period. External assets are held as domestic monetary reserves, or reserves against bank liabilities and thus not entirely available for covering a deficit.

Ireland's long-term investment position. A complete picture of Ireland's long-term investment position cannot be readily estimated from official statements. The balance of payments, for example, shows changes in a country's position on an annual basis over a period of time; it does not show the total amounts at a given point in time. Because of statistical errors, even for purposes of showing changes from year to year, the values included in the statement must be considered rough estimates at best. In addition, while the difference between current account debits and credits are necessarily equal to the net capital inflow or outflow, the latter includes both long- and short-term movements. Short-term movements, in turn, partially reflect action of the banking system which, in the process of accommodating private traders, increases or decreases its holdings of short-term claims.

During the five-year period 1962-1966, Ireland's total deficit on current account amounted to approximately £125 million or an average of £25 million each year. The deficit reflected the impact of a change in external assets of the banking system, a change in Irish holdings of stocks and bonds in foreign countries (disinvestment), and a flow of new capital into the country as foreigners purchased Irish stocks and bonds. (Preliminary figures indicate a £10 million current account *surplus* for 1967.)

At the beginning of 1962, external assets of the banking system and of departmental funds amounted to £224.5 million; at the end of 1966, they amounted to £253.5 million which meant a gain (a short-term outflow) of £29 million or almost £6 million on average each year. Accordingly, the net inflow from other sources (the non-bank or non-monetary sector) must have amounted to approximately £31 million each year on average for the period (1962-1966).

The volume of private capital movements in and out of Ireland is closely related to the level of domestic capital formation, exports and general economic activity. As noted in Chapter V, the net capital inflow has generally been the largest during periods when Ireland's exports and gross national product were growing most rapidly. It would appear that capital is relatively mobile between countries and that external investors, particularly the British, are responsive to shifts in the marginal efficiency of capital in Irish export industries.

The significance of external capital in Ireland's economic expansion can be shown by expressing it as a share of gross domestic capital formation (GDCF). According to projections made for 1970 in the *Second Programme for Economic Expansion*, GDCF (which includes both public and private investment) would be financed as follows: current savings, 57 per cent; depreciation provisions, 35 per cent; and external capital, 8 per cent. The actual average figures for the period 1960-1966 were as follows: current savings, 53 per cent; depreciation provisions, 36 per cent; and external capital, 11 per cent. The first two components grew at a relatively stable rate (in absolute terms) during the period. External capital behaved erratically during the same years, ranging from £1.2 million in 1961 to £42.0 in 1965.[4]

In addition to a wide variation in the volume of capital movements, there are also year-to-year changes in the composition of such movements (as indicated in Table II-1). However, a general idea of the composition of the capital inflow might be gained by examining the figures for 1966. For 1966, the net capital inflow, including both short- and long-term movements, amounted to £16.1 million. A major source was the external subscription to central government and local authority issues, prize bonds, and exchequer bills; the value of £18.4 million for 1966 was unusually high in comparison with other recent years. Net receipts from the International Monetary Fund amounted to about £ 4.1 million, reflecting Ireland's use of drawing rights on that institution. Public and private issues by companies amounted to about £5 million; other direct investments in Ireland, £14.4 million; and other inflows, £8.3 million. Transactions in securities through Irish stockbrokers and bankers have averaged about £17 million each year, both buying and selling, but a net outflow of about £2 million occurred in 1966. Finally, external assets of the banking system increased about £29 million (a capital outflow).

The accumulated volume of outside investment in Ireland has been estimated in several different studies. One estimate made in 1961, which was admittedly highly speculative in nature, placed the foreign ownership of Ireland's industrial capacity at about 30 per cent of the total value.[5]

A second study of the capital structure of industry was based on a questionnaire completed by Irish firms. The authors of this study recognized the limitations of their approach and the need for cautious interpretation of data. They determined, however, that for the manufacturing firms responding to their survey, about 34 per cent of paid-up capital was held by individuals and companies residing outside of the State. The highest proportions of paid-up capital held by foreigners were in the chemical and chemical products industry, metals and engineering and other manufacturing industries.[6] According to a more recent estimate, 80 per cent of *new private* investment during the first six years of planning (1958-1963) represented external financing.[7]

Despite the substantial capital account surplus, Ireland's receipts from income from investment abroad and external profits, etc., as listed in the balance of payments statistics (line 15, Table II–1) have *exceeded* payments on the same account, and by a growing amount, since prior to World War II. One reason is that the Irish have invested substantial amounts abroad, largely in Britain, in past years. For example, during World War II, Ireland ran a relatively large capital account deficit, much of which represented an increase in sterling claims held by Irish banks. Because of past investments of this nature, interest and profits continue to accrue to Irish residents from overseas sources.

The balance of payments item 'income from investment abroad and extern profits, etc.' cannot be used to estimate the past volume of long-term capital movements. In the first place, it contains payments and receipts for *both* short- *and* long-term capital. A second factor which must be considered is that the content of certain balance of payments accounts may be somewhat misleading. As defined in the June 1952 issue of the *Irish Trade Journal and Statistical Bulletin*, income from investment abroad and extern profits also includes certain banking, insurance and industrial transactions. For example, an adjustment is included for certain export trading concerns incorporated outside the state; the merchandise exports of these concerns are included as a credit entry in the merchandise account, and are also debited along with net receipts from sales in Ireland, less expenses in this country.

The Irish government is making extensive efforts to attract external capital especially in those instances in which the result is to increase productive capacity in the export industries. An advantage of this approach is that the foreign exchange needed to service the obligation is generated by the investment itself thus reducing the possibility of a subsequent balance of payments problem.

Incentives have been provided both to Irish and to foreign firms to promote widespread industrialization and to make Irish goods competitive in world markets. As an illustration, there has been a complete exemption of income tax and corporation profits tax on profits arising from new exports. In addition, depreciation allowances have been liberalized, and grants and loans have been available to firms particularly in instances where new capital formation took place, where the investment project was located in areas of rural underemployment, and where the result would be to make an enterprise competitive even under conditions of free trade.

In addition, the government places virtually no exchange controls either on the inflow of capital or on the subsequent repatriation of earnings. One exception is that the purchase of unlisted securities and non-urban land by foreigners requires prior approval. As a result of the unrestricted exchange transactions, the tax incentives, and a general climate conducive to private enterprise, it has been possible for the government to attract investment from firms in Great Britain, continental Europe, North America and Japan.

Sources of external capital. The Second Programme for Economic Expansion calls for outside capital of at least £16 million each year. In addition to the private capital markets of Great Britain, Europe and the U.S. which can be utilized by the government and private firms of Ireland, some long-term investment funds can be secured through several official agencies. The most important possibilities include the International Bank for Reconstruction and Development (IBRD or World Bank), the International Finance Corporation (IFC), the U.S. Export-Import Bank, and the European Economic Community's European Investment Bank (assuming Ireland becomes a member of the Community).

Ireland joined the IBRD along with the International Monetary Fund in 1957. As implied in the title of the institution, the IBRD provides long-term loans for reconstruction and development purposes. Loans are made only to governments or under a government guarantee. In practice, the Bank has extended a large share of its loans to an official lending agency in the borrowing country which, in turn, provides smaller-sized loans to private firms. From the borrowing country's point of view, the advantages of borrowing from the IBRD are circumscribed in that the institution will cover only the foreign exchange requirements for a given investment project. In addition, the interest rate charge is relatively high if compared with that which might be paid on loans from other official institutions. The reason for the high interest charge is that the IBRD seeks to avoid competing unfairly with private lenders in commercial capital markets.

At the time Ireland joined the IBRD, it was expected that she would secure long-term capital from the institution. However, a large share of the Bank's loans has been made to the low-income countries and Ireland has yet to obtain financial assistance from the institution. By and large, the bulk of financial resources has been provided to the developing economies of Africa, Asia and Latin America; however, IBRD loans were extended to such countries as Australia, Belgium, Denmark, Italy, Japan and Norway during the period 1960-1967.

The over-all objective of the International Finance Corporation (IFC), which came into existence in 1956, is to complement the activities of the World Bank. Thus the IFC provides financial assistance only to private firms in member countries. Generally the Corporation will provide no more than half of the resources needed to complete a given project but usually will not undertake financing involving less than $500,000. It makes funds available in the form of long-term loans and also in exchange for a non-voting security of the firm; accordingly, it avoids any voice in the direct management of a firm. After the enterprise is firmly established with its projects, the IFC expects to sell its holdings to interested parties in the host country. In a sense, the IFC hopes to perform a catalytic role in the development of private industry.

Ireland became a member of the IFC in 1958, but has yet to secure a loan from the organization. It would appear that she normally would not have recourse to the Corporation's financial assistance, particularly as long as private capital continues to be available from other sources on reasonable terms.

Should Ireland become a member of the European Economic Community, she would be eligible for loans from the European Investment Bank (EIB). The EIB possesses capital subscribed by member states (the equivalent of $1,000 million) and also is authorized to borrow funds in world capital markets; it can provide assistance for projects for the less developed regions, for modernization or adaptation of existing facilities, or for creating new undertakings which would facilitate the progressive development of the Community. The EIB is not to compete with private lending institutions. The interest rates charged have generally ranged from 6 to 7 per cent, and the Bank has provided only a part of the total capital needed for a given project. In its operations through the end of 1966, it had approved loans in member states totalling $572 million involving over 100 projects. Well over one-half of the loans have been made for projects in Italy, which is probably the least developed and industrialized of the member states. Loans have also been approved for projects in Greece and Turkey, both of which are associate members of the Community, and also for projects in the Associated African States.

Thus Ireland, which is less industrialized than most of the existing full members of the Community, could probably become an important borrower from the EIB. Even as an associate member of the Community, Ireland might be eligible for its financial assistance if the precedent established with Greece and Turkey is followed elsewhere.

Ireland would, of course, be expected to subscribe to the Bank's capital resources. Although the exact amount would be determined by negotiation, present subscriptions of the smaller members of the Community might be suggestive of Ireland's obligation. The contributions of Luxembourg, the Netherlands, and Belgium are .20 per cent, 7.15 per cent, and 8.65 per cent, respectively, of the total. For each country, 25 per cent of the capital was paid during the first years of the EIB's operations; the remaining 75 per cent is subject to call to the extent necessary to meet the Bank's obligations.

The Export-Import Bank of Washington (Ex-Im Bank), an agency of the U.S. government, is a source of medium- and long-term credit and loan guarantees. It provides funds for financing exports and for projects designed to promote economic reconstruction or development. Loans are extended to American or foreign firms and to foreign governments but the project must be economically sound and self-liquidating.

An obvious characteristic of the Ex-Im Bank's operations is the effort to promote U.S. exports. Generally the Bank will cover only the foreign exchange requirements involved in the completion of a given project. In addition, the Bank's loans are 'tied'; i.e., the proceeds must be spent on items procured in the U.S.

As an example of Export-Import Bank operations, Aer Lingus signed a contract in 1967 for the purchase of two aircraft. Aer Lingus will cover part of the cost from its own resources, the U.S. aircraft company will extend a certain amount of credit, and the remainder will be borrowed from the Export-Import Bank.

1. See, for example, Central Bank. *Report of the Central Bank of Ireland for the Year Ended 31st March, 1965.* Dublin: 1965, pp. 8-10.
2. In the 1920's, the United States took the inconsistent position of demanding that foreign countries repay their debts, and also pursuing a restrictive commercial policy which made it increasingly difficult for foreign countries to earn dollars.
3. Jan de Weille. 'Export Fluctuations and Debt Service Problems: A Short-Term Indicator' in Dragoslav Avramovic, *et al.*, *Economic Growth and External Debt* (International Bank for Reconstruction and Development). Baltimore: Johns Hopkins Press, 1964, pp. 125-130.
4. Figures derived from *Review of 1966 and Outlook for 1967.* Dublin: Stationery Office, 1967, p. 31.

5. Edward Nevin. 'The Irish Economy in 1960,' *The Irish Banking Review*. September, 1961, pp. 12-26.

6. E. W. Henry and Louis J. Heelan. 'Capital in Irish Industry,' *Journal of the Statistical and Social Society of Ireland*. Vol. XXI, Part I, 1962-63, pp. 135-190.

7. Loraine Donaldson. *Development Planning in Ireland*. New York: Frederick A. Praeger, 1965, pp. 36-39.

100

UNIVERSITY OF VICTORIA
LIBRARY
Victoria, B. C.

CHAPTER VIII

BENEFITS OF TRADE

A country striving for a higher rate of economic growth must employ its resources as efficiently as possible. The factors of production – land, labour, and capital – must be used where specialization along certain lines of activity is possible and where the value of their output is greatest. Perhaps the major advantage of international trade is that it permits the factors of production to specialize and to be used where their output is maximized.

The basic argument for international specialization and exchange of goods and services reflects the work of such early English writers as Adam Smith, David Ricardo, and John Stuart Mill. The formulations of these writers were quite abstract; nevertheless, the basic principles embodied in their theories continue to be accepted generally as the foundation for international trade theory.

Comparative costs: John Stuart Mill. The analysis provided by John Stuart Mill (1806-1873) is a fairly complete statement of the principle of comparative costs.[1] Mill, as his predecessors, developed a two-country, two-product model. He also assumed that labour costs of production or supply factors determined prices or exchange values in domestic trade. He then used the following example:

> In England's domestic trade, production conditions are such that 10 yards of broadcloth exchange for 15 yards of linen;
> In Germany's domestic trade, production conditions are such that 10 yards of broadcloth exchange for 20 yards of linen.

Trade between the two countries could be beneficial to both if England specialized in broadcloth production and Germany in linen production.

In England, 10 yards of broadcloth exchange for 15 yards of linen and accordingly she would benefit from foreign trade only if *more* than 15 yards of linen could be secured in exchange for 10 yards of broadcloth. In Germany, 10 yards of broadcloth exchange for 20 of linen; accordingly, she would gain from foreign trade only if it were possible to give up *less* than 20 yards of linen to get 10 yards of broadcloth. Mill concluded that there is a basis for a mutual gain from trade between the two countries; the exchange ratio would be such that 10 yards of broadcloth would exchange for 15 to 20 yards of linen (i.e., if the exchange ratio were between 10 : 15 and 10 : 20). Only within this range would a mutual advantage exist and provide both countries with an incentive for trade.

Mill concluded that domestic cost and supply factors set the outer limits within which international exchange ratios must fall. However, demand conditions determine the actual point within this range at which the exchange ratio would settle. If, for example, England's demand for linen imports were relatively intense, the exchange ratio might settle at 10 : 16; if Germany's demand for broadcloth imports were relatively intense, the ratio might be set at 10 : 19.

With international specialization, countries gain because of the higher level of world output. According to Mill, the gain each country derives from trade is reflected in the difference between the rate at which goods exchange for each other internally (in the absence of external trade) and the rate at which they exchange in foreign trade. Assume, for example, a 10 : 17 external exchange ratio. England with a 10 : 15 domestic cost ratio would get 17 yards of linen for 10 yards of broadcloth; this would represent a net gain of 2 yards of linen for every 10 yards of broadcloth exported. Germany, with a 10 : 20 domestic cost ratio, would obtain 10 yards of broadcloth for every 17 yards of linen, and accordingly would save 3 yards for every 17 exported. Or, at an external ratio of 10 : 19, England would gain 4 yards of linen for every 10 yards of broadcloth exported; Germany would save 1 yard of linen for every 19 exported.

Mill believed that the abstractness of his model did not make it any less realistic. He concluded, for example, that regardless of the number of countries and products analyzed, the same essential principles apply as in trade between two countries and with two commodities.

Mill and other early writers asserted that there was always a basis for trade between countries. As long as the domestic exchange ratio differed from one country to a second, there was a cost advantage to be derived in specializing in items which could be produced most efficiently, and importing items which are produced least efficiently.

Even the relatively 'poor' nations are able to export some type of commodity. This is because the 'rich' nations find it advantageous to import certain items which, while they could be created domestically, would divert resources away from more productive uses. As an illustration, Great Britain could today possibly expand its domestic production of cattle and other agricultural commodities. But the cost would be high for Britain as it became necessary to shift resources away from the production of motor cars, machinery and other items which she can manufacture relatively efficiently. The U.S. could become virtually self-sufficient except for a variety of minerals and tropical foods. However, a move toward greater self-sufficiency on the part of the U.S. would mean that some resources, now devoted to the production of goods with a high technological content, must be used in a less efficient fashion producing items previously imported.

Mutual interdependence: Bertil Ohlin. Early writers on the theory of international specialization were occupied largely with the gains to be derived from trade. The work of the Swedish economist Bertil Ohlin has directed attention more toward the basic *causes* of international trade.[2] Ohlin believed that the causes of trade are related to regional factor endowments and that trade between regions is similar to trade between nations. He also stressed the mutual interdependence of income, demand, factor and commodity prices, and factor movements as they relate to interregional and international trade.

The immediate cause of trade is that of price differentials; an item can be purchased from a foreign source at a more favourable price than from a domestic source. What then causes the price differential? Ohlin based his explanation on two circumstances. The first is the unequal endowment of the factors of production – land, labour, and capital – in different regions or nations of the world. Some regions have an abundant supply of natural resources but capital is relatively scarce; others may have an abundant supply of capital with labour the relatively scarce factor. The second circumstance contributing to commodity price differentials is the varying proportions of the factors of production embodied in commodities. Some commodities require a relatively large amount of capital but little land for their production; still other commodities might be labour-intensive.

Ohlin concluded that a region or a nation would produce and export goods which embody the factor of production which is relatively abundant; it will import items which embody large quantities of its relatively scarce factor of production. A labour-abundant country will export labour-intensive commodities and import capital- or land-intensive items. A country rich in farm land and poor in capital goods will tend to export agricultural commodities and import finished goods and services. A free flow of goods and services will enable each region to use its available factors most effectively and thus to expand total production. The comparative advantage possessed by a given country depends largely upon its factoral endowment in comparison with that of other countries. The principle of comparative costs is thus reinforced by the description of factors which cause price differentials to arise.

Dynamic considerations of trade. The composition of a country's exports must be considered within a dynamic framework. As a nation advances economically and experiences growth, the structure of its foreign trade alters to correspond with a shifting pattern of resource endowment and comparative advantage. A factor of production becomes either more or less scarce over time in comparison with other factors within the country; this in turn affects the type of output for which the country is best suited.

A country at an early stage of development typically enters world commerce as an exporter of natural resource intensive commodities – minerals, foodstuffs and other raw materials; it imports a wide range of finished goods and services. But as the country advances it generally becomes more industrialized and develops a *technologically-skilled* labour force. Growth in investment usually proceeds at a more rapid pace than developments in other sectors. As a result, capital becomes a relatively more abundant factor of production. Thus a country's comparative advantage gradually changes over time; the natural resource content of exports is narrowed, the capital and technology content is broadened.

The long-term composition of trade is affected not only by supply or production considerations, but also by income and consumption factors. That is, with economic growth, per capita incomes rise and a shift occurs in the demand for goods and services or in the composition of commodities consumed. Some goods and services become relatively more important as a portion of total spending; they are income *elastic*. Other goods become relatively less important; they are income *inelastic*.

Thus the composition of a country's imports and exports changes over time reflecting the combined influence of the supply and the consumption effects. A country not only produces a different set of commodities more efficiently, but also consumes a somewhat different set of commodities.

A change in the composition of Irish trade, especially exports, is quite evident in recent years, even for relatively short periods of time. For example, in 1962, industrial exports represented 32 per cent of total exports; agricultural produce and other exports, 68 per cent. By 1967, industrial exports had increased to 41 per cent of the total; remaining types had declined to 59 per cent.

Terms of trade. Mill's version of the principle of comparative costs is useful for showing the benefit from trade, but only in an abstract way. Efforts have been made in more recent years to develop techniques which can be applied in a practical way to show the gains from trade. One of these techniques involves the use of the concept 'terms of trade.'

The terms of trade are used to compare a certain aspect of a country's exports (price, volume, or value) with a certain aspect of its imports. The [concept 'commodity terms of trade' is used to compare the price relationship between a country's exports and imports in an effort to determine the trend in gains from external trade. Thus the commodity terms of trade are identified as

$$\left(T_c = \frac{P_{e1}}{P_{eo}} \middle/ \frac{P_{i1}}{P_{io}} \right)$$

with T_c representing the commodity terms of trade; P, a price index; the subscripts e and i for exports and imports respectively; and the subscripts 1 and o for the given year and the base year. A country's commodity terms of trade are said to be 'favourable' or improving if export prices (P_e) rise in relation to import prices (P_i) – a rise in T_c – or 'unfavourable' or worsening if the opposite happens. Stated in another fashion, a given volume of exports will buy a greater volume of imports as a country's terms of trade become more favourable or improve; a smaller volume of imports, as the terms become unfavourable.

Although the commodity terms of trade are useful as one measure of a country's position in world trade, they must be interpreted carefully and used with extreme caution. Generally it would appear that an improvement in a country's terms of trade would necessarily be desirable. This need not be the case, however, if for example the external demand for the country's exports is so price elastic that the *value* of exports, reflected in foreign exchange earnings, actually falls. Under such circumstances, the country gives up less of its exports to acquire a given volume of imports, but may also find it more difficult to earn foreign exchange to buy imports. Thus the country may be either better off or worse off.

It is also possible that a country's commodity terms of trade worsen but that there is also an increase in domestic efficiency in producing exports. Under such circumstances, the cost of imports may be no higher than before in terms of domestic resources actually used.

Finally, it should be noted that the figures derived in measuring the terms of trade are subject to all of the statistical problems involved in the construction of any price index. This includes the selection of a base year for which trade patterns and prices are not distorted, the weighting of commodities to reflect their relative importance in total trade, and shifting the composition of the index to reflect new types of commodities. Furthermore, a country's

TABLE VIII–1

EXTERNAL TRADE: VOLUME, PRICE, AND TERMS OF TRADE, 1955-1967[a]

Year	Imports Volume	Imports Price	Exports Volume	Exports Price	Terms of trade Commodity	Terms of trade Income
1955	108	104.1	95	101.4	97.4	92
1956	93	106.1	98	95.9	90.4	89
1957	89	111.9	117	97.6	87.2	102
1958	100	107.0	114	100.1	93.5	107
1959	110	104.7	110	104.0	99.4	109
1960	114	106.6	130	102.2	95.9	125
1961	131	107.7	156	101.0	93.8	146
1962	137	107.6	149	101.9	94.7	141
1963	152	109.4	165	103.9	94.9	157
1964	171	110.4	177	109.8	99.5	176
1965	178	112.9	174	110.9	98.2	171
1966	178	112.9	189	112.9	100.0	189
1967	188	112	218	114	102	222

[a]Base year of 1953. Figures for 1967 are provisional.

Source: Figures derived from Central Bank. *Report of the Central Bank of Ireland for the Year Ended 31 March 1967*. Dublin: 1967, p. 134; *Review of 1967 and Outlook for 1968*. Dublin: Stationery Office, 1968, pp. 48, 51.

past experience with its terms of trade is not necessarily a good indication of the future trend; projections relating to the more basic conditions of supply and demand are needed for this purpose. Subject to these qualifications, a knowledge of a country's terms of trade is useful in that they reflect the relation between the prices a country pays for imports and receives for exports.

Perhaps a more useful measurement is a second index which combines the commodity terms of trade with trade volume indices in an effort to reflect changes in a country's capacity to import. This measurement – the income terms of trade – in no way reflects the gains from trade. The income terms of trade are equivalent to

$$T_y = T_{c1} (Q_{e1}/Q_{eo})$$

with T_c representing the commodity terms of trade; Q, a quantity index; the subscript e, exports; and the subscripts 1 an o the given and the base year respectively. The income terms of trade might also be described as an index representing the imports secured from exports actually shipped out of the country. The income terms of trade might improve (i.e., T_y might rise) if the price of exports (P_e) rises, or if the quantity of exports (Q_e) rises, or if the price of imports (P_i) falls, assuming in each case that the other variables remain constant. The income terms of trade are useful in showing trends in a country's ability to import, but are not suggestive of the gain or loss from such trade.

Irish terms of trade. Changes in the price and volume of Ireland's exports and imports and her commodity and income terms of trade (with 1953 the base year) are shown in Table VIII-1 for the years 1955 through 1967. During this period Irish export prices appear to have fluctuated somewhat more than import prices; this, in part, is the result of a greater variety of imports than of exports. Ireland's commodity terms of trade were unfavourable especially during the periods 1956-1958 and 1960-1963 as compared with a 1953 base year, but recovered in 1964 and 1965 approximately to the 1953 level. In 1966 the index stood at 100, indicating no improvement or deterioration as compared with the base year 1953.

Ireland's income terms of trade are also shown in Table VIII-I. Although her capacity to import declined somewhat in 1955 and 1956, it expanded in succeeding years and by 1965 was about 70 per cent greater than in 1953. A significant increase also occurred in 1966 and 1967. The increase was due largely to the expansion in the volume of exports since the price of exports and of imports rose almost equally by the end of the period.

Tariffs and other trade restrictions. According to international trade theory, the free flow of goods and services across national boundaries is essential for the most efficient use of world resources. In practice, all countries use tariffs and other trade barriers in varying degrees of restrictiveness in the belief that it accomplishes one or more of several different objectives. While trade barriers can be justified on economic grounds on a temporary basis for certain purposes, the permanent use of such restrictions reflects a willingness to sacrifice efficiency for some other objective—national self-sufficiency, maintenance of a national identity, the welfare of a special interest group, or stability of domestic economic activity.

As a basis for assessing the arguments for trade protection, one fundamental consideration must be emphasized: an economy cannot in the long-run export goods and services, unless it also imports goods and services. In the short-run, a differential between the value of commodity exports and the value of imports may be covered by grants or capital movements. In the long-run, one country's exports can be paid for by other countries only by the first country's purchases from abroad. Thus policies of protectionism must be recognized as damaging to existing export industries – industries which are probably using resources efficiently if they are competing in world markets.

A second basic consideration is that tariffs generally result in higher consumer prices. Insofar as buyers of goods and services bear the burden of a tariff duty on imports, or purchase items produced domestically in an inefficient fashion, their real incomes are reduced.

A wide range of techniques, instruments and policies are used to implement a country's commercial program. Tariffs represent one of the oldest forms of protection, but there are also quotas, exchange controls and embargoes. Campaigns and legislation to 'buy domestic products' are more subtle, but may be equally effective in protecting domestic industry.

Arguments for trade restrictions. One of the oldest pleas for tariff protection is the *infant industry argument*. According to this argument, there are certain firms and industries which could compete both in domestic and world markets if they were given an opportunity to become firmly established. Tariff protection is to be employed on a temporary basis to provide new firms an opportunity to eliminate organizational inefficiences or to take advantage of any potential economies of scale. In time, the cost of production and also prices can be lowered sufficiently to compete in world markets. Although this argument has merit, there is the practical difficulty of determining which firms or industries can operate in the long-run without tariff protection.

It is sometimes argued that it may be desirable to exclude certain types of imports from countries in which the wage rates are relatively low. Domestic labour must be protected from *cheap foreign labour*. This reasoning has been applied particularly to imports from many of the labour-abundant Asian countries. The fallacy in this argument relates to the fact that wages are only one of the several costs of production. Highly-paid labour combined with a substantial amount of capital in one country may be able to produce as effectively and inexpensively as workers in a second country who receive a lower wage rate but have a smaller amount of capital equipment at their disposal. If wage rates are high in a particular country, it is because worker productivity is high and able to compete in industries in which a comparative advantage is attained.

It is also argued that protection is needed to *expand domestic employment*. This argument is particularly appealing for industries and regions in which the level of unemployment and underemployment is relatively high. However, it can be argued that because of the dual nature of trade, the protection of certain industries with the objective of increasing their employment will in the long-run contract the level of employment in the export industries. When a country reduces its imports, other countries are less able to buy its exports; as a result, production and employment in the external sector decline. In the short-run, however, tariffs may increase domestic employment by switching demand from foreign to domestic goods. As various types of resources, including labour, are transferred into the import-competing industries, an additional number of workers come to be employed, but in a less efficient fashion.

Another argument in favour of tariffs is that such levies represent a convenient *source of government revenue*. Revenue from this source can be collected inexpensively and there is little chance of evasion. In assessing this argument, a distinction must be made between tariffs whose major function is to acquire revenue and those whose function is to protect domestic industry. A tariff which is completely protective (in the sense that it prevents any imports) provides no revenue. A tariff which provides a substantial amount of revenue must be low enough to permit importing and thus may not afford a high degree of protection to domestic firms.

Customs duties represent one of Ireland's more important sources of revenue, accounting for about 25 per cent of total Exchequer receipts. About two-thirds of total customs duties, in turn, are from levies on tobacco imports. Other dutiable items which provide a substantial amount of revenue include motor vehicles, mineral oil, clothing and apparel.[3]

Another argument for trade protection is that it promotes *national self-sufficiency and security*. Accordingly, a country does not move into a vulnerable position in which serious damage can accrue to the domestic economy should supplies be cut off as a result of war or antagonistic policies of a trading partner; the danger would be particularly great and the argument would appear to have some merit in instances where an importing country secures a large share of its supplies of a particular commodity from one external source. However, in opposition to this argument, it might be noted that virtually all types of commodities are essential for the well-being of a society. To be completely secure and to avoid the risk of import supplies being stopped and causing serious damage, a country would have to be self-sufficient in virtually all types of production. National self-sufficiency and security may be an acceptable objective. But to what extent should it be sought at the expense of productive efficiency? The argument has perhaps even less merit for the small economy with a narrow natural resource base. To institute the production of a certain item within the country does not lessen the dependence on the world economy if it remains necessary to import raw materials or other components for its manufacture.

It is argued that protection must be devised to prevent *sporadic dumping*. Dumping is the practice of selling goods at a lower price in a foreign market than in the home market. Dumping may occur if a firm attempts to exploit elasticities of demand which it believes differ from one market to a second; it may occur if a firm wishes to dispose of a large inventory without upsetting its usual markets; it may be used as a predatory device to eliminate competition. There is general agreement that sporadic dumping has an adverse economic impact on the importing country insofar as it disrupts production conditions in that country. Because of the smallness of the Irish market, there has been a major concern that action of this type by foreign firms might easily force an entire domestic industry out of business.

In assessing the impact of the practice, it must be recognized that it is *sporadic* or occasional dumping which causes damage to an importing country. If dumping is *persistent*, or occurs over an extended period of time so that consumers and producers are assured of a continuing supply of that commodity at a low price, then it is difficult to show that this adversely affects the importing country. In fact, the very gain from trade involves the importation of items at favourable prices.

A problem with the uneconomic and disruptive sporadic dumping is that the practice cannot be easily eliminated through protective tariffs without curbing the normal inflow of commodities. The practice must be detected relatively soon, and to be effective, remedial action must be taken almost immediately. In 1967, member countries of the General Agreement on Tariffs and Trade adopted a uniform anti-dumping code. The features of this code are examined in Chapter X.

Trade restrictions have also been advocated as a basis for *promoting domestic diversification and stability*. It is generally believed that a country which exports a limited variety of commodities and which conducts a large share of her trade with one or a few countries is more likely to experience instability in its foreign trade prices and terms of trade than other countries. Insofar as a lack of diversification contributes to price instability in the foreign trade sector, it also contributes to instability and uncertainty of prices, income and employment in related sectors in the domestic economy.

Despite a high *geographical* concentration of external trade –

both exports and imports – as well as a high export *commodity* concentration, Ireland's export and import prices, and commodity terms of trade have not been unusually unstable, at least according to one study. In a study of 44 countries by Michael Michaely, Ireland is ranked second in geographic concentration of exports, eighth in geographic concentration of imports for the year 1954. However, for the years 1948 through 1958, Ireland's *import* prices varied only 3.9 per cent, while for a group of 36 countries for which data were available, the mean variation was 10.4 per cent. For the same years, Ireland's *export* prices varied only 5.8 per cent as compared with a mean variation of 7.7 per cent for all countries. Consequently, Ireland's *terms of trade* varied only 4.2 per cent whereas the mean variation for the 36 countries was 9.0 per cent.[4]

Michaely's study would seem to suggest that the extreme geographic and commodity concentration which has characterized Ireland's trade in the past has not resulted in unusually adverse conditions pertaining to external trade prices. Presumably the major type of commodity Ireland exported (live animals) as well as the market conditions in her major trading partner (Great Britain) were factors contributing to this stability.

Irish commercial policy. Irish development policy, which has been 'outward looking' in recent years, is in sharp contrast to the autarkical policies of the early 1930's. External tariffs have been reduced by 10 per cent on each of two occasions in the last several years; recent active participation in the General Agreement on Tariffs and Trade is also evidence of a long-term policy of free trade.

A major difficulty of the Irish economy in world commerce is that many of the items which can be produced and exported by Ireland – particularly agricultural commodities – are also items whose production is protected and heavily subsidized in many potential importing countries. The governments of virtually all industrialized countries have introduced policies which have retarded the flow of resources out of areas in which a comparative disadvantage has developed. As a result, little success has been achieved in liberalization of trade barriers on farm commodities. For example, at the most recent session of the General Agreement on Tariffs and Trade, major tariff reductions were made on industrial products, but little could be agreed upon with respect to agricultural commodities.

While existing foreign markets for Irish agricultural exports are likely to remain the major source of foreign exchange earnings, new attention is being directed toward industrial exports. Thus many types of industrial exports are being subsidized, directly and indirectly, in the hope of acquiring and retaining overseas market outlets. Ireland's 'outward looking' development policy is unusual among those countries which are today specializing in the production of agricultural or primary commodities. Most of these countries have moved in the direction of planned 'import substitution' or autarcky – policies which are reminiscent of Ireland in the 1930's.

The Puerto Rican case. Although most industrializing countries, unlike Ireland, are pursuing restrictive commercial policies and import substitution as a strategy for growth, one exception is Puerto Rico. The Puerto Rican case is of interest because the economy in certain respects parallels Ireland's and because Puerto Rico in the 1940's shifted from an emphasis on the export of primary commodities to one on the export of manufactured commodities. In both instances, the new development programs are based on the possibility of a potential comparative advantage in a new line of activity rather than clinging to historic comparative advantage or pursuing a restrictive trade policy.

Puerto Rico's situation and new program are not unlike Ireland's: the existence of unemployed labor which offers a potential comparative advantage in certain types of output; inability to rely extensively on domestic markets to achieve economies of scale; preferential treatment in a large external market; use of generous concessions to attract outside capital; use of subsidies and direct assistance rather than protection to stimulate industry; and, a growing share of aggregate output directed to outside markets. Puerto Rico's increase in total output is exceptionally high; according to one estimate, her per capita real income increased 50 per cent during the 11 year period 1946-47 through 1956-57.[5]

Ireland's subsidization of new industrial exports reflects an assumption of a potential comparative advantage in certain lines of manufacturing activity. Ireland possesses the basis for increased industrialization including the essential infrastructure – health and educational facilities, as well as transport, harbour and power facilities. Ready access to British and other capital markets will facilitate the expansion of productive capacity in the export industry. Ireland's comparative-advantage approach to development will, of course, induce major structural change within the economy as tariff protection is withdrawn from inefficient firms and as other firms are afforded new external market opportunities.

1. John Stuart Mill. *Principles of Political Economy.* Edited by W. J. Ashley, London: Longman's Green and Co., 1920, pp. 574-606.

2. Bertil Ohlin. *Interregional and International trade*. Cambridge, Mass: Harvard University Press, 1933.
3. *Finance Accounts* (For the Financial Year 1966-67, ended 31st March, 1967). Dublin: Stationery Office, 1967, pp. 4-9.
4. Michael Michaely. *Concentration in International Trade*. Amsterdam: North-Holland Publishing Company, 1962.
5. For an excellent description of Puerto Rico's use of external trade to promote development, see Joseph E. Haring. 'External Trade As an Engine of Growth,' *Economia Internazionale*. XIV (1961), pp. 97-118

CHAPTER IX

EMIGRATION

International economics is concerned not only with the flow of goods, services and capital among countries, but also with the movement of people across national boundaries. The study of migration, however, is more complex because in addition to being an economic phenomenon, it has social, cultural, and psychological dimensions.

The Irish rate of emigration has been among the highest in the world. In the early 1840's, the population of the Republic was about 6.5 million; by 1966, it had declined to 2.9 million. The high rate of emigration is largely a manifestation of social dissatisfaction with the relatively low level of income and rate of economic growth which has characterized the Irish economy. Employment and income opportunities elsewhere, particularly in the United States and later in Great Britain, have led to a rate of emigration which in many years has exceeded the natural rate of growth of the population. However, according to preliminary reports of the latest intercensal period (1961-1966), the natural increase in population (excess of births over deaths) amounted to 10.3 per cent while net emigration during the period amounted to 5.9 per cent (Table IX–1). Average annual net emigration amounted to about 16,770 during the period, the lowest figures for the post World War II years.

Much of the emigration since the end of World War II has been to Great Britain, in part because there is a complete freedom of movement between the two countries. The Irish worker needs no passport or identity card to secure a job in Britain; in many ways it is as easy for the Irish worker to obtain employment in a British city as it is in another Irish city.

Theoretical implications of emigration. The economic implications of population movements for the country of emigration depend upon conditions relating to employment, productivity, and emigrant remittances, among other things. In general, labour will move from areas where it is abundant to where it is scarce, thus reducing the extent to which wages are low in the first area. In most instances, if labour moves for economic reasons or in response to a wage differential, the marginal productivity and average income of remaining workers will rise, thus improving the well-being of the latter. In instances where a departing worker was

TABLE IX-1
AVERAGE ANNUAL RATE OF NET EMIGRATION
1926–1966

Period	Rate
1926–1936	5.6
1936–1946	6.3
1946–1951	8.2
1951–1956	13.4
1956–1961	14.8
1961–1966	5.9

Source: Central Statistics Office. *Census of Population of Ireland 1966*
(Preliminary Report). Dublin: Stationery Office, 1966, p. 12.

unemployed or underemployed (a low marginal output) or where his job is taken over by someone else who would otherwise be unemployed, the economic gains to the country of emigration are apparent. Since there is little or no decline in total output, per capita income would be higher as there is a smaller population to share in total output.

The impact on the economy is not likely to be favourable, however, if the emigrant is a highly-skilled or a professional worker. If such persons had actually been employed, their departure would remove a productive element from the country and may adversely affect per capita income.

In general, it can be stated that total output or aggregate GNP will decline as emigration occurs insofar as the marginal productivity of departing workers exceeds zero. However, maximization of *per capita* rather than *aggregate* income may be a more appropriate objective for a given economy. Accordingly, a more important consideration is that the departure of workers whose marginal productivity is less than average (above average) will result in an increase (decrease) in per capita income of the remaining workers. If a government were to pursue a goal of maximization of per capita income and could institute a selective emigration policy, the major criterion applicable to individual workers would relate to their contribution to total output.

Impact on age composition. Empirical evidence suggests that emigrants are likely to be in the most productive age brackets and for this reason could represent a potential loss to a country, depending upon their marginal output. Emigration also has an impact on the age composition of the remaining population. A large percentage of Irish emigrants are in the potentially employ-

TABLE IX-2

AGE STRUCTURE OF IRISH POPULATION, 1946, 1951, AND 1961

		Age Group			
Year	0–14	15–44	45–64	65 and over	Total[1]
1946	27.5	41.8	18.8	10.5	100
1951	28.9	41.0	19.4	10.7	100
1961	31.1	36.4	21.2	11.2	100

[1]Because of rounding, totals may not equal 100.

Source: Central Statistics Office. *Statistical Abstract*. (Recent issues.) Dublin.

able age brackets and, as a result, the share of Ireland's population in this age group (15-64) is lower than that of most other countries. Or it could be stated that the share in the dependent age groups (0-14 and 65 or over) is higher than that of other countries. The age structure of the population for 1946, 1951 and 1961 is shown in Table IX-2. The major general observation to be made is that the share of the population in the age group 15-44 is declining while the share of all other age groups is rising. The decrease in the share of the potentially most productive age group represents the continuation of a trend going back to the 1840's. However, the *increase* in the share of the age group 0-14 represents the *reversal* of a *declining* trend from the 1840's until the beginning of World War II. The percentage point gain in the 'young' group (0-14) since 1946 roughly equals the gain in the 'old' group (45 and over).

Emigrant remittances and capital movements. An important advantage to the country of emigration is the flow of emigrant remittances as workers send funds to their families, relatives and friends in the country from which they departed (Chapter II, Table II-1, line 17). Such funds augment the savings of the recipient country and, equally important, provide it with access to foreign exchange and external resources. Such amounts are likely to be greatest if workers emigrate by themselves and remit funds to their immediate families. They are likely to be lowest if emigration occurs by family units. For Ireland, the amount of receipts from remittances has ranged from £13 million to £15 million each year in the 1960's.

The significance of this inflow is more meaningful if compared with that of other countries of emigration. A study submitted to the World Population Conference estimates emigrant remittances as a percentage of imports and as a percentage of national income for four countries for the years 1960, 1961 and 1962. Emigrant remittances as a percentage of *imports* were as follows: Italy, 8 to 9 per cent; Spain, 8 to 10 per cent; Greece, 14 to 22 per cent; and Portugal 6 to 10 per cent.[1] The respective figures (estimated) for Ireland for the same years were somewhat lower, ranging from 5 to 6 per cent.[2]

Emigrant remittances as a percentage of *national income* were as follows: Italy, 1.6 to 1.9 per cent; Spain, 0.7 to 1.4 per cent; Greece, 3.5 to 4.7 per cent; and Portugal, 2.0 to 2.6 per cent.[3] The respective figures (estimated) for Ireland were 2.1 to 2.4 per cent.

Offsetting, in part, the inflow of emigrant remittances as a gain to the country of emigration are the capital outflows which accompany departing persons. Such capital movements represent a use of foreign exchange which might be employed for imports or alternative uses. The average amount of capital which accompanies each person is unknown, but is likely to vary considerably with relatively small amounts being taken out by the young, single worker, to relatively larger amounts for the older family units. The Irish government places no restrictions on amounts which an emigrating family can take if they are moving to another Sterling Area country. If the move is outside the Sterling Area an upper limit of £5,000 is placed on the sum which can be automatically transferred to the new country.

Economic growth with unlimited supplies of labour. One of Ireland's major resources has been an abundant supply of labour. Labour is, in a sense, the most important factor of production and if available under appropriate conditions can be expected to facilitate the growth process.

A model of economic growth based on an unlimited supply of labour and on the transfer of this labour within an economy from the agricultural to the industrial sector has been advanced by W. Arthur Lewis. Lewis assumes that disguised unemployment (or underemployment) exists in the agricultural sector and that there is an autonomous increase in demand for manufactured commodities from the industrial sector. Thus profits rise in industry, investment is expanded, and workers are drawn into industry from agriculture. However, wages in industry remain constant as long as unemployment prevails in agriculture. The constancy of wages leads to higher industrial profits, these continue to be reinvested and as a result the growth process continues.[4]

Employment shifts in the post-World War II Irish economy are shown in Table IX–3 which indicates employment in the primary

TABLE IX-3
EMPLOYMENT SHIFTS, 1946-1966

| | Employment | | | Change in employment | |
Sector	1946	1956	1966	1946–1956	1956–1966
Agriculture, forestry and fishing	567	430	330	— 137	— 100
Industry	229	269	289	+ 40	+ 20
Services	432	426	423	— 6	— 3
Out of work	71	63	64	— 8	+ 1
Total	1299	1188	1106	— 111	— 82

Source: Figures derived from National Industrial Economic Council. *Report on Full Employment.* Dublin: Stationery Office, 1967, p. 15; *Review of 1966 and Outlook for 1967.* Dublin: Stationery Office, 1967, p. 36.

sector, industry and services for the years 1946, 1956 and 1966. It is apparent that in neither of the ten-year periods (1946-1956 or 1956-1966) was there sufficient growth in the industrial (and service) sector to absorb the workers released from agriculture, forestry and fishing. The result, which does not correspond with the Lewis model, was a decline in the size of the labour force as workers and their families emigrated abroad at an average rate of about 20,000 per year (a rate which, however, has slackened considerably since the early 1960's).

The failure of the economy to approximate the Lewis model of growth is probably the result of at least two factors: inadequate expansion in demand for manufactured commodities and failure of the wage rate to remain steady. Of course, in the Lewis model, unlimited supplies of labor are not a sufficient or an initiating cause of economic growth; rather they are to be considered in the nature of a permissive condition. The slow growth in demand for industrial commodities may be in part the consequence of a restrictive policy of 'import substitution' through the 1930's and 1940's, a policy which was probably inappropriate for an economy as small as Ireland's. In addition to a small domestic market, industry was unable to gain access to foreign markets on a substantial scale.

The failure of the wage rate to remain constant as specified in the Lewis model reflects a combination of factors. One writer suggests that wages are likely to rise most rapidly in countries where: (a) there are close geographical, political, and cultural ties with industrial countries, including freedom of movement between them; (b) the government attempts to follow enlightened social policies; and (c) the trade union movement is strong.[5] These factors are characteristic of the Irish economy and probably contributed to the general increase in wage rates.

Exports and emigration. As noted in Chapter VII, a country exports items embodying large amounts of the abundant factor of production; it imports items embodying large quantities of the scarce factor of production. Thus one result of trade is that increased exports lead to a greater demand for the abundant factor which in turn becomes relatively less abundant. With increased imports, the scarce factor becomes relatively less scarce. Consequently the difference in the relative scarcities of factors of production as well as inequalities in factor prices are reduced among countries. Accordingly, free trade at least partially weakens the inducement for factor migration by causing both commodity and factor prices to move toward equality among trading areas. In this manner, free commodity trade may occur instead of factor movements among countries.

The use of export subsidies is also likely to reduce emigration particularly if the result of such payments is to develop industries operating at a potential comparative advantage and using the abundant factor of production as a major input. The use of tariffs and a restrictive commercial policy, however, will reduce the flow of imports as well as exports. As a consequence, the abundant factor of production will receive a relatively lower rate of return and, if it is a mobile factor, there will be increased incentive for it to migrate.

It is not likely, however, that free trade will completely eliminate commodity and factor price inequalities. The existence of transportation costs of commodity trade is the most obvious impediment. There are also market imperfections – inadequate knowledge and occupational and geographical immobility – which preclude a complete equalization. An additional consideration is that although increased exports result in a greater utilization of the abundant factor of production, this factor may not be an adequate substitute for the scarce factors of production in certain types of production because of relatively fixed factor proportions (or fixed technical coefficients). If labour, for example, is the abundant resource but is not a good substitute for capital or land in the productive process, wage rates may remain lower than in other countries and there will be incentive for it to migrate.

Movements of the factors of production may also serve to offset or reduce the flow of commodity trade. The reason is that as factors move from countries where they are relatively abundant to where they are scarce, inequalities in relative factor endowments among countries are reduced. As a result, comparative cost differentials are narrowed and there is less scope for profitable trade.

It has been noted that both labour and capital move freely across Irish boundaries, especially with respect to Great Britain. If a high degree of mobility of all factors were assumed, an analysis of international specialization based on factor endowments would be less relevant, since it would follow that productive factors would shift to areas which were conducive to productive efficiency and the less productive areas would be uninhabited. This suggests the extremely complex nature of forces affecting the flow of trade. Of major importance is a recognition that the factor endowment existing in a given country is both a cause and a result of commodity trade.

Despite the possibility of a relatively high degree of mobility of one or more factors across national boundaries, there are several elements which contribute to the uniqueness of regions with respect to relative factor endowment – thus providing a basis for trade. A basic consideration is that certain factors, notably natural resources – land, climate, rainfall, minerals – are immobile and generally must be exploited where they are found. In addition, the utilization of immobile resources requires a full complement of factors of production including those which might otherwise be mobile. A second consideration is that the agricultural and industrial complex existing in a given country may reflect a development and use of resources of an earlier period when there was an immobility of commodities or factors between countries. Finally, it is generally believed that on balance non-economic forces contribute to an immobility of certain productive agents, particularly labour. Thus labour is not likely to emigrate unless there is a decided differential in income returns abroad.

Government policy on emigration. Although it is generally agreed that the relatively poor performance of the Irish economy has contributed to a movement of workers to other countries, some writers suggest that the line of causation also runs in the other direction. That is, since workers can find employment in other countries, there is less pressure on the government of the domestic economy to initiate the action and the changes needed to expand internal employment.[6] Thus an important economic implication of emigration may be a reduction in the incentive to improve conditions at home.

The Irish government has condoned emigration and for the most part the restrictions that do exist are those imposed by countries of immigration. Nevertheless, the situation in which Irish persons feel they must emigrate to achieve an adequate scale of living has been deplored, and efforts are being made to create conditions in which Irish families feel that domestic income and opportunities are adequate rewards.

Because of the size and openness of the Irish economy, it has been assumed that the traditional monetary and fiscal policies, usually most successfull in coping with cyclical unemployment, are not completely appropriate nor adequate for eliminating 'structural' unemployment. That is, employment opportunities cannot be raised significantly by simply increasing demand to match existing capacity. Instead, productive capacity itself must be expanded especially in industry in accordance with sales opportunities at home and abroad to create additional job opportunities. The industrial capacity which must be created involves combining existing labour with additional machinery, equipment, plant and buildings.

The expansion of industrial capacity and employment opportunities requires capital resources as well as market outlets and consequently requires a long-term program. Thus one of the major objectives in the *Second Programme for Economic Expansion* is 'to secure the progressive reduction of involuntary emigration so that by 1970 net yearly emigration will be reduced to 10,000 at most.' An expansion in industrial exports will create additional job opportunities in the export sector; it is in this sense that commodity trade can be considered a substitute for the migration of labour.

There is evidence, however, that with a change in attitude on the part of employers and employees and perhaps greater market opportunities, employment could be raised somewhat with little or no increase in capital equipment. The reason is that industries traditionally run one eight-hour shift per day. If a second and possibly a third shift could be operated by certain firms, then employment of workers would double or triple with no increase in capital equipment. The fuller use of plant and equipment might also lower per unit production costs.[7]

Two factors are likely to reduce the flow of Irish emigration and the high unemployment rate in coming years. The first is the liberalization of world trade which will provide a greater opportunity to utilize the abundant factor of production as export trade is expanded. The second is the capital inflow which, insofar as it contributes to an accumulation of machinery, equipment and other capital resources, will result in a full complement of productive factors capable of adjusting more readily to market demands.

Yet it is not likely that even a relatively successful program to create domestic employment will eliminate Ireland's net emigration in the near future. The move to Great Britain and to the U.S. has been a part of Irish society for generations. It is not only a generally-accepted pattern but also has tended to perpetuate itself as persons are brought to new areas by workers who preceded them.

Ireland and the EEC. A decision of Ireland to enter the European Economic Community (EEC) would very likely lead to a greater movement of Irish workers to the European member countries. The EEC provides for a relatively free change of residence of workers and their families in response to job vacancies in other member countries. Movement within the Community is encouraged in that workers retain their social security rights as they shift from one member country to a second; they have the right to settle permanently and to participate in trade union activities. Movement is also encouraged as a result of financial assistance from the European Social Fund for vocational retraining and resettlement purposes.

Participation by Ireland in the EEC will affect the labour force in other ways particularly with respect to social systems and also remuneration of men and women workers. Article 119 of the EEC's Rome Treaty specifies that member states are to apply the principle of equal pay for equal work as between men and women. This condition was to have been met by the end of 1964 but, although a good deal of progress had been made in this respect, had not yet been completely realized by mid-1968. Ireland, as a full member of the EEC, would be expected to comply with this provision after a transition period.

The Treaty of Rome (Article 117) also calls for the harmonization of social systems. Ireland's expenditure on public social security benefits as a percentage of GNP is lower than that for most European countries.[8] It is possible that, as a member of the EEC, Ireland would find it necessary to alter and perhaps provide a more liberal system, to the extent necessary that the type of system does not in itself adversely affect the movement of people and commodities within the Community. However, major immediate changes would not be required in Ireland's system. An important immediate objective is that a citizen of one country working in a second country be accorded treatment equivalent to that already provided workers in the second country. In addition, there is to be an exchange of views and information on policies among member countries in order that there be an ultimate harmonization as individual systems are developed and improved.

122

1. Giuseppe Parenti. 'Role of Emigrants' Remittances in the Economic Development of European Countries,' summarized in United Nations, *World Population Conference, 1965*. 1966, pp. 138-150.
2. Central Statistics Office. *Irish Statistical Bulletin*. June 1965, p. 75.
3. Parenti. *op. cit.*
4. W. Arthur Lewis. 'Economic Development With Unlimited Supplies of Labor,' *Manchester School*. May 1954, pp. 131-191.
5. John Pincus. *Trade, Aid and Development* (Council on Foreign Relations, Inc.). New York: McGraw-Hill Book Co., 1967, p. 168.
6. See for example J. F. Meenan. 'Eire,' *The Economics of International Migration* (Edited by Brinley Thomas). International Economic Association. London: Macmillan & Co., Ltd. 1958, pp. 77-84; and National Industrial Economic Council. *Report on Full Employment*. Dublin: Stationery Office, 1967, pp. 112-114.
7. See National Industrial Economic Council. *Report on Full Employment*. Dublin: Stationery Office, 1967, pp. 98-100.
8. P. R. Kaim-Caudle. *Social Security in Ireland and Western Europe*. Dublin: The Economic Research Institute, June 1964.

CHAPTER X

ARRANGEMENTS FOR TRADE LIBERALIZATION

Ireland's decision to participate more actively in world trade has led to an interest in a number of arrangements with other countries in which one of the major objectives is that of facilitating a freer flow of goods and services across national boundaries. The scope of the different arrangements varies significantly, both in terms of geographical area and in terms of objectives.

In this chapter, four of these arrangements will be examined: the General Agreement on Tariffs and Trade; the Anglo-Irish Free Trade Area, the European Free Trade Association and the Organization for Economic Co-operation and Development. In the following chapter, a fifth arrangement, the European Economic Community, will be considered.

Ireland has been a member of the Organization for Economic Co-operation and Development since its inception in 1960; she became a full member of the General Agreement on Tariffs and Trade in late 1967. Along with the United Kingdom she has established the Anglo-Irish Free Trade Area. Ireland does not participate in the European Free Trade Association, but has applied for membership in the European Economic Community.

The importance of certain of these areas for Irish exports and imports is indicated in Table X–1 which shows the direction of trade for 1967. Although over half of Ireland's trade is with the United Kingdom, this share is likely to decline if she becomes a member of EFTA, the EEC, or if trade barriers are reduced significantly on a world-wide basis.

The General Agreement on Tariffs and Trade. The arrangement which perhaps has done most to promote international trade liberalization since the end of World War II is the General Agreement on Tariffs and Trade (GATT). GATT is essentially an arrangement whereby most of the major trading nations meet in sessions every three to four years to negotiate on a multilateral basis for the reduction of tariffs. The first GATT session occurred in 1947 with 23 participating countries; at the sixth and most recent session, the 'Kennedy Round,' which was completed in 1967, 38 countries actually made concessions although a total of 54 countries attended.

A key feature of GATT is the multilateral negotiation, an innovation introduced during its first session, which is in contrast to the

TABLE X–1
DIRECTION OF IRISH TRADE, 1967

Area	Percentage distribution Imports	Exports
United Kingdom	50.2	72.0
Other EFTA countries	3.8	1.1
Total EFTA countries	54.0	73.1
EEC countries	14.6	8.5
Other European OECD countries	1.0	.6
Dollar countries	10.8	10.8
All other areas	17.8	4.4
Re-imports and temporary domestic exports	1.8	2.6
Total	100.0	100.0

Source: *Review of 1967 and Outlook for 1968.* Dublin: Stationery Office, 1968, p. 57.

preceding bilateral negotiations between pairs of countries. Under a multilateral system of bargaining a concession – usually a tariff reduction or a 'binding', an agreement not to raise a tariff – will be extended by one country to a second country in exchange for an equivalent concession; eventually, however, these concessions are extended to all other participating countries. In other words, multilateral bargaining involves negotiations on the part of several countries with the most-favoured-nation principle in operation. With the most-favoured-nation principle in effect, a concession extended by a country is generalized, or applied to all countries. As a result discriminatory tariff preferences are avoided.

GATT has also proved useful over the years as a medium through which trade disputes between member countries have been settled. If, for example, a country invokes an escape clause and withdraws a concession it had made at an earlier date, then the exporting countries adversely affected are entitled to withdraw an equivalent concession. In mediating such disputes, GATT attempts to ensure fair treatment for all parties and to hold the number of concessions withdrawn to a minimum.

In certain respects, the GATT-sponsored Kennedy Round was one of the more important of the several sessions which has been undertaken. The significance of the session cannot be easily summarized in quantitative terms. According to some reports tariffs on industrial commodities were lowered by an average of about 35 per cent. These changes go into effect gradually and generally will not be fully implemented until 1972. However, in the absence of a knowledge of such factors as demand and supply elasticities for traded commodities, the extent to which initial tariffs were excessively protective, and the relative importance of particular commodities in world trade, the implication of the reductions cannot be determined with any degree of accuracy for exports and imports.

Tariff reductions secured under GATT in the Kennedy Round do reflect a continued willingness on the part of most major trading countries to work toward the liberalization of world trade, particularly in industrial commodities. In terms of technique, the Kennedy Round was unusual in that it marked the first effort to negotiate on a 'linear' or across-the-board approach; earlier sessions involved bargaining on an item-by-item approach. The major area in which trade restrictions were relaxed but slightly was in agricultural commodities.

Another important achievement of the Kennedy Round was the adoption of a uniform Anti-Dumping Code. Fear of the adverse effects of dumping has been great in Ireland and other small economies which are particularly vulnerable to such practices. For purposes of the Code, dumping is defined as the introduction of a product into the commerce of another country at less than its normal value, if the export price is less than the comparable price of the product when destined for consumption in the exporting country. The Code provides that anti-dumping duties may be imposed, but only when there is factual evidence that dumped imports are clearly the principle cause of material injury or threat of material injury to a domestic industry. The Code goes into effect either on 1 July 1968 for each country which has accepted it, or at a later date as it is accepted by each country.

Ireland and GATT. Ireland's membership in GATT was not secured until 1967. An application first made in 1961 was suspended during the time Ireland was initially seeking membership in the European Economic Community. In the interval, however, she maintained an observer status and had, in fact, been extended the tariff concessions that member countries exchanged.

Ireland acquired full membership in GATT early enough to participate in the tariff reductions negotiated during the Kennedy Round. These reductions, as noted previously, were more significant than those of earlier rounds, particularly with respect to industrial commodities. Although Ireland will benefit as a result of easier access to markets for industrial exports, a more immediate gain in terms of larger markets for agricultural exports was not realized because of the failure of the contracting parties to make

126

significant progress in liberalizing restrictions on trade in farm commodities.

Irish industry will be able to export more easily to many countries for which trade barriers will be less restrictive. At the same time, it will face increased competition in domestic markets. Ireland had made two over-all 10 per cent tariff cuts on a unilateral basis in preceding years (January 1963 and January 1964); these were taken into consideration at the Kennedy Round. The major new concessions by Ireland involved a guarantee not to impose or raise tariffs on a wide range of items. For a small number of items Irish tariffs were reduced.

Increased competition will also develop as a result of Kennedy Round tariff reductions in countries where Ireland has enjoyed preferential tariff treatment in the past, particularly Great Britain but also Australia and Canada. The preferential treatment will be narrowed somewhat and Irish producers will face increased competition from firms in third countries. The arrangement affected most directly in this respect will be the Anglo-Irish Free Trade Area.

By becoming a member of GATT, Ireland is afforded the certainty of the benefits of tariff concessions extended by other countries, concessions which on some occasions in the past had been extended only at the courtesy of existing members. Participation in the organization does not obligate Ireland to lower trade barriers at future sessions although it is true that the benefits she receives in terms of access to outside markets will be of the greatest immediate value if she is willing to offer concessions to other countries. Ireland will also have the use of GATT as an international forum in which to air any grievances which might arise as a result of commercial policies of other member countries.

Anglo-Irish Free Trade Area. By far the greatest share of Ireland's trade has been with the United Kingdom (Table X–1). Ireland has been a major supplier of live animals, food and beverage; she has imported a wide variety of items from the U.K., including machinery and components and vehicle parts. Ireland's trade with the U.K. has declined in relative terms since the 1930's. However, this share is likely to rise as a result of a more comprehensive trading arrangement between the two countries, particularly if they are unwilling or unable to participate in the European Economic Community (EEC) or if the world-wide trend toward freer trade under GATT should come to an end.

In 1965, Ireland concluded a new Anglo-Irish Trade Agreement with the United Kingdom which would lead to a free trade area between the two countries and which is designed to promote struc-

127

tural changes in the two countries compatible with membership in the European Economic Community. Under previous Anglo-Irish Agreements (1938, 1948 and 1960), many categories of Irish exports were provided duty-free access to the United Kingdom market. Ireland, in turn, accorded preferential tariff treatment to goods imported from the United Kingdom.

The 1965 Agreement was far more extensive in its impact on commerce between the two countries. The major provisions of the Agreement are as follows:

(i) store cattle, sheep and lambs, all major Irish exports, are guaranteed completely free access to U.K. markets. Previously the U.K. could restrict the quantity if this was deemed necessary 'in the interests of orderly marketing'. Ireland will also benefit more fully from guarantee payments made under the fat-stock guarantee program generally available to British producers. British import quotas on Irish butter are also to be gradually expanded;

(ii) all other Irish agricultural commodities, and horticultural and fishery products are accorded relatively unrestricted access to U.K. markets. Access is duty free and it is restricted in quantitative terms only insofar as necessary to be compatible with orderly marketing and the provisions of certain international commodity agreements;

(iii) any remaining duties on Irish industrial imports into the United Kingdom are to be eliminated. Most industrial exporters already enjoyed free access to British markets; textiles were the major category affected by the 1965 Agreement;

(iv) Ireland is to remove import duties gradually over a ten-year period, beginning in July 1966, on most items imported from the United Kingdom. Excluded from the duty-free provision are jute, several agricultural commodities and products with a large agricultural content. On 1 July 1967, protective duties on British goods were reduced by 10 per cent;

(v) Ireland is also to remove quantitative restrictions, particularly with respect to industrial goods, which have previously applied to British imports.

Certain safeguards are incorporated into the Agreement. The Irish government may impose quotas for a specified period of time or postpone tariff removal during the early years of the transition period if there is an appreciable rise in unemployment in a sector of industry or a region.

A comprehensive review of the operation of the Agreement is to be made in 1970. If at that time any industries or regions are experiencing or expect to experience severe difficulties of a permanent character, the two governments will consider the possibility of postponing tariff removal or even excluding the products from the Agreement. However, the extent to which this 'escape clause' may be used is limited. The exceptional treatment can apply to no more than 3 per cent of the value of all imports of Ireland from Britain. Thus it cannot be considered as an alternative readily available to the firm which fails to adjust to meet foreign competition.

The 1965 Agreement has important implications for Irish agriculture and industry. In the first place, trade with the United Kingdom, especially in store cattle, sheep and lambs, will be placed on a more *certain* basis as access to this market cannot be easily or arbitrarily terminated. Secondly, the agreement assures Irish exporters of both agricultural and industrial commodities of a *larger* market in the U.K.

Finally, and equally important, the 1965 Agreement subjects Irish firms, especially in industry, to the competitive forces of a broader market area. Irish firms must be competitive and efficient if they are to survive. Although increased efficiency is a prerequisite for survival, certain features of a free trade arrangement, such as greater opportunities for economies of scale and lower costs on imported inputs (as duties are removed), may provide an opportunity for reducing per unit costs of production. The long-run potential gain to Irish firms, however, is a degree of efficiency which permits them to compete more effectively in world markets.

Thus the Anglo-Irish free trade arrangement must be considered both an opportunity and a challenge to Irish producers. Efficient firms and industries will find profit opportunities expanded; other firms shielded by protective tariffs and selling in the domestic market will find it necessary to adopt new techniques or make other modifications if they are to withstand the competitive pressures of British industry. The *gradual* removal of tariffs and quantitative restrictions on imports of British goods is designed to give Irish producers ample time to undertake the necessary change in their purchasing, producing and marketing technique.

The European Free Trade Association. At one stage during the existence of the Organization for European Economic Cooperation (OEEC), a number of European countries explored the feasibility of a free trade area to include all OEEC countries. It proved impossible to agree on the type and degree of integration; the European Economic Community came into existence, and by May of 1960, a second trading arrangement, the European Free Trade Association (EFTA), had been established. The original seven members of EFTA were Austria, Denmark, Norway, the United Kingdom, Portugal, Sweden and Switzerland; Finland became associated with the group in 1961 and her status approximates that of a full member.

EFTA is a less ambitious and possibly a less permanent organization than the EEC. Its major and basic feature is the gradual removal of trade restrictions on industrial products within the grouping. The initial step to reduce barriers occurred in July 1960 when internal barriers were lowered 20 per cent. Rapid progress was made on this provision and by the end of 1966 virtually all tariffs and quotas were eliminated. Tariff reductions were planned to coincide with the internal tariff reductions made by the EEC, but actually the EFTA countries were first to complete the objective.

Members of EFTA, unlike the EEC, maintain their respective national tariffs against outside countries and accordingly do not need to develop a common external tariff. It is this feature which permits Britain to maintain tariff preferences with the Imperial Preference System and a free trade association with Ireland; if Britain were a member of the EEC, she could not retain such arrangements without special exceptions.

A unique problem faced by EFTA was that, because a uniform external tariff was not established, importers might avoid the duties of a high-tariff country by importing items initially into a low-tariff country. To meet this problem, evidence is required from exporters that at least half of the value of a product shall have been added in an EFTA country before it can be shipped freely throughout the region.

EFTA is basically designed to encourage internal trade in industrial goods; it has not attempted to develop a common agricultural program. However, while tariff barriers are not being eliminated on agricultural and fishery products, some are being classified as industrial products and accordingly will be traded freely.

Ireland in EFTA. As an alternative to other regional groupings, Ireland could participate in EFTA. EFTA involves a market area of approximately 100 million people, a total GNP of $170 million and per capita national income of $1,400. With the exception of Britain, remaining members have small populations, although larger than Ireland's. In terms of natural resources, size and certain other factors, many of the member countries are not unlike Ireland.

The incentive for Ireland to enter EFTA is reduced by virtue of a situation of free trade with Britain, its largest member. Approximately 72 per cent of Ireland's exports are to the United Kingdom; 1 per cent to other EFTA countries. Approximately 50 per cent of her imports are from the United Kingdom; 3.8 per cent, from other EFTA countries.

However, the basic shortcoming of EFTA from the Irish point of view is the virtual exclusion of agricultural commodities from the free trade arrangement. If Ireland is to derive immediate gains from such an association, overseas markets for agricultural products would have to be opened. Free trade within EFTA is limited to industrial products; Irish participation in EFTA would lead to intensive competition from industrial concerns in EFTA, but would not create a significant market for any Irish exports.

Organization for Economic Cooperation and Development. In 1960, membership in the Organization for European Economic Cooperation (OEEC) was expanded to include two non-European countries, the United States and Canada, and the name of the arrangement was changed to the Organization for Economic Cooperation and Development (OECD). The OECD presently has 21 members; it includes the member countries of EFTA and the EEC, as well as Canada, Greece, Iceland, Ireland, Japan, Spain, Turkey and the United States.

The OECD operates on a cooperative basis to achieve such objectives as the expansion of world trade on a multilateral, non-discriminatory basis, and the promotion of full employment and economic growth both in member countries and in developing non-member countries. In general, the OECD serves as a forum in which member countries can discuss and exchange views on economic matters of mutual interest; it accumulates and disseminates statistical data and information on economic policies of member countries; it attempts to develop common policies for member countries with respect to such matters as external trade, aid for developing countries, and manpower and social policies.

Any decisions made by the OECD Council require the unanimous approval of member countries. However a member country can abstain from voting and thus not affect the unanimity rule. In many instances, the Council renders recommendations rather than decisions; the result is to exert pressure on member countries to comply on a voluntary basis.

The OECD does not directly attack problems of world trade, finance or investment as would such specialized institutions as GATT, the IMF, or the World Bank. Its chief importance is that it represents a cooperative effort on the part of the major industrial countries of the non-Communist world to find solutions to economic problems of mutual concern.

Certainty of trade. As the various organizations and arrangements pursue their objective of trade liberalization, the Republic of Ireland will gain access to broader markets both within the context of regional arrangements (the Anglo-Irish Free Trade Area and possibly the European Economic Community) or within a world-wide context (the General Agreement on Tariffs and Trade). In either case, the result is to provide Ireland with some of the same advantages in production (e.g., economies of scale) as those held by the larger nations.

A point emphasized at the 1957 meeting of the International Economic Association in an examination of the role of foreign trade for the small economy centered on a type of risk characteristic of foreign trade which is not present in domestic trade. The risk is related to possible abrupt change in commercial policies on the part of importing countries.

Because of changes in quotas, tariffs or exchange rate policy or even the fear of such change, exporters may be unwilling to rely extensively on foreign markets as a source of income. Because commercial policies can be changed overnight and consequently a foreign market lost, exporting firms may not seek outside markets in an aggressive fashion. Ireland experienced a problem of this nature, for example, when Britain imposed a 15 per cent import surtax in 1965.

In at least one respect, the regional groupings, in that they contribute to trade patterns which are more durable or permanent, may be more suitable for the small country.[1] If a country is to invest a significant share if its resources to develop or expand its export industries, it must be assured that its major trading partners do not prohibit or even partially restrict imports in some arbitrary fashion. The Anglo-Irish Free Trade Area and the EEC are based on certain provisions which render internal trade liberalization a permanent feature. Extensive unilateral commercial policies on the part of a member country would probably lead to the dissolution of the arrangement.

Tariff concessions extended under GATT can be withdrawn, although not easily, through certain escape clauses and, as a result, a degree of uncertainty prevails. The U.S. in particular, at least until 1962, was frequently criticised for using one or more of its 'escape clause' provisions. The complaint has been voiced that if a foreign firm succeeds fully in selling in U.S. markets, its government is likely to invoke the escape clause in order to restrict imports.

Competitiveness of Irish industry. Whether Ireland continues to implement the provisions of the Anglo-Irish Free Trade Agreement, whether she becomes a member of either the EEC or EFTA or whether significant tariff reductions are made through GATT,

Irish industry will feel the impact of foreign competition as trade barriers are removed. One result of the tariff protection instituted in the 1930's has been a degree of inefficiency on the part of many firms. Reports of the Committee on Industrial Organization indicate that for many industrial concerns buildings were unsuitable, obsolete techniques and machinery were being used, management was unenterprising, the variety of production was excessive, and marketing arrangements were inadequate.[2] Major changes will have to be undertaken if the inefficient firms are to survive the force of external competition; according to one estimate in early 1966, existing industrial import tariffs fell largely in the $33\frac{1}{3}$ to 50 per cent range.[3]

Impact of free trade on specific industries. In view of the high degree of protection which has been afforded certain Irish industries, there has been concern over the trend toward free trade and its impact on Irish industrial concerns. Accordingly, in 1961, the government of Ireland established the Committee on Industrial Organization (CIO) with representatives from various branches of Irish industry. The major objective of the CIO was to make a comprehensive survey covering 26 industries of the Irish economy to determine what measures would be necessary to adapt Irish industry to conditions of freer trade and more intensive competition. Similar studies were undertaken by the Department of Agriculture for four industries, and the Industrial Reorganisation Board (IRB) for 24 industries each representing one or a small number of firms.

On the basis of these studies and other estimates made by the CIO, the conclusion was drawn that the net decline in employment caused by a complete freeing of trade barriers would be about 10,000 in all manufacturing industries provided adaptation measures were taken by these industries. (Total manufacturing employment at the time amounted to about 150,000.) In the absence of adaptation measures the net decline in employment would be two to three times as great.

Some of the major industries affected most adversely by the freeing of trade, assuming adaptation measures were taken, would be as follows: Cotton, Linen and Rayon; Leather; Leather Footwear; Miscellaneous Clothing and Accessories; and Iron and Steel Manufactures.

According to the survey team, one activity, the Motor Vehicle Assembly industry, would be forced out of production with the freeing of trade; this industry exists only because of tariffs which are sufficiently high to prohibit importation of virtually all fully-assembled vehicles.[4]

The conclusions of these surveys must be interpreted in a

cautious fashion. They clearly point to the need for the implementation of adaptation measures if much of Irish industry is to become or remain competitive. These studies do not imply, however, that total employment in Irish industry will decline in coming years as economic expansion occurs and as Ireland, along with other countries, moves toward a free trade policy. In fact, as noted in Chapter I, it is estimated that with growth and development under the Second Programme, industrial employment would increase by almost 3 per cent each year for the period 1964-1970.

Changes in the foreign trade sector must be related to shifts in the structure of employment which characterize the growth pattern of any dynamic economy. Some industries expand, others contract, in conjunction with changes in technology, the development of new products, and new profit opportunities. When implemented in a gradual fashion, the impact of free trade on employment need not be particularly great when compared with all of the forces which affect productive activity.

Efforts on the part of the Irish government to assist in the adjustment process of the private sector are not unique among the industrialized countries. Members of the European Economic Community, for example, provide grants and loans to accommodate industrial adjustment. Financial assistance is provided by the U.S. government for the specific purpose of easing the burden which falls on those American workers, firms and industries adversely affected by increased imports.

Irish establishments and economies of scale. The potential for improving the competitiveness of a given enterprise initially operating within the confines of a small insulated economy hinges in part on the possibilities of economies of scale. For some types of commodities, the average cost of production can be minimized only after a large volume of output is achieved – too large in fact to be absorbed in the domestic economy. Hence the dependence on external markets. The firm may also be able to secure some types of inputs – raw materials and capital goods – from external sources at a lower price.

Because of the small size of the domestic market, it is frequently noted that Irish manufacturing establishments have less of an opportunity to take advantage of economies of scale than do firms in larger countries; further, Irish firms will presumably become more competitive as they gain access to foreign markets and are able to realize lower unit costs as output expands. As a practical matter, empirical evidence is not sufficiently consistent to prove the existence of significant economies of scale.[5] Recent studies suggest that, with a few exceptions, moderate-sized firms even in

134

small and poor countries can achieve the full possible economies of scale; the exceptions would be those firms producing various types of vehicles and transportation equipment. For example, there seems to be no evidence of an increase in the average size of industrial establishments since the 1930's in the U.S. and Canada, among other countries. Other studies of British firms suggest that the size of firms and efficiency in given industries were not necessarily related.[6]

A comparison of the size of Irish manufacturing establishments (in terms of employment) with those of other European countries is also revealing. Studies which compare the size of manufacturing establishments for Ireland, Britain, Federal Republic of Germany, France, Norway, Sweden and Switzerland indicate that generally they are no smaller in Ireland than in the remaining countries.[7]

Thus there are no clear indications that Irish firms will acquire a size advantage as opportunities are improved in foreign markets. Economies of scale may exist to a certain extent, but other factors affecting costs may be more important than the size of the market. Of major importance are ready access to various types of raw materials at favourable prices, a willingness to utilize existing capital equipment to the fullest extent, and attitudes and institutions which encourage and reward the development of entrepreneurial activity.

In addition, certain *external* economies may develop and be available to firms; with wide-spread industrial expansion, power, transportation and communications may be supplied at a lower per unit cost. The spread of industry may also contribute to a larger supply of trained and skilled labour as well as the development of managerial talent and technological knowledge. All of these factors serve to lower production costs.

Other aspects of external markets. By operating within the framework of larger markets in industrialized countries, the firm as well as the entire small economy may gain through what is termed 'learning effects' and the improvement of human resources. As a result of participation in external commerce, people acquire modern horizons, new working habits, and technical skills. The learning process not only increases the economy's productive capacity, but also makes it more flexible and capable of transforming to meet new market opportunities.[8]

The firm in the small economy, however, will be at a disadvantage in certain respects. It appears that generally it is easier for a firm to develop and test products initially in a large home market and subsequently expand into outside markets. The firm in the small economy must of necessity develop outside markets at an earlier stage; because of the possible need for overseas marketing arrangements and because of an unfamiliarity with consumer tastes, customs, labour practices, and the legal environment, developing a foreign market may involve a risk which is too high for the small firm. The 1967 *Annual Report* of the Irish Export Board (Córas Tráchtála) indicates that of approximately 2,000 firms producing articles which might be exported, only 700 – approximately one-third of the total – were actually engaged in the export business.

Some if the difficulties of entering the foreign market can be avoided, however; many firms, for example, contract with firms located in the foreign market to undertake the distribution of the product.

The government has introduced a number of steps to induce industrial efficiency. Import quotas have been liberalized and tariffs on industrial imports were reduced by 10 per cent in January 1963 and again in January 1964. In July 1967, protective tariffs on British goods were reduced by 10 per cent. Adaptation grants and loans are available to firms for modernisation of plant and equipment, expansion of productive capacity, and establishment of new lines of production. However, assistance of this nature is available only if there is evidence that it would make the firm competitive under conditions of free trade. Through 1964 grants and loans had been approved for a wide range of industries: textiles, wearing apparel, paper and paper products, printing, chemicals, drugs, engineering, machinery, cutlery, hollowware and electrical appliances. Financial assistance is also available to promote managerial training. Since emphasis is being placed on industrial exports, the government offers a wide range of facilities to stimulate foreign shipments including relief from income tax and corporation profits tax on profits derived from increased exports, grants for market research, and technical assistance for firms entering the export business.

1. G. Marcy. 'How Far Can Free Trade and Customs Agreements Confer Upon Small Nations the Advantages of Large Nations?' *Economic Consequences of the Size of Nations* (E. A. G. Robinson, ed.). London: Macmillan & Co., Ltd., 1963, pp. 265-281.
2. Committee on Industrial Organization. *Final Report*. Dublin: Stationery Office, 1965.
3. Organization for Economic Cooperation and Development. *Ireland*. Paris: 1966, p. 26.
4. Results of the surveys are included in Committee on Industrial Organization. *Final Report*. Dublin: Stationery Office, 1965.
5. For a survey of the literature, see J. Jewkes. 'Are the Economies of

Scale Unlimited?' *The Economic Consequences of the Size of Nations* (Austin Robinson, ed.). London: Macmillan & Co., Ltd., 1963, pp. 95-116.

6. *Ibid.*

7. See David O'Mahony. *The Irish Economy* (Second ed.). Cork: Cork University Press, 1967, pp. 31-32; and W. A. Johr and F. Kneschaurek. 'Study of the Efficiency of a Small Nation: Switzerland,' *The Economic Consequences of the Size of Nations* (Austin Robinson, ed.). London: Macmillan & Co., Ltd., 1963, pp. 54-77.

8. A discussion of the 'learning effects' is provided by Donald B. Keesing. 'Outward-Looking Policies and Economic Development,' *Economic Journal.* June 1967, pp. 303-320.

CHAPTER XI

THE EUROPEAN ECONOMIC COMMUNITY

The institution which has probably had the greatest impact on Irish thought relative to future economic progress and growth is the European Economic Community (EEC or Common Market). Ireland aspired to be a member of the EEC by 1970 at the latest but expected that in the interim internal agriculture and industry must be sufficiently rationalized to compete effectively within the framework of a broader market.

Nature of the EEC. The EEC was not the first effort at regional cooperation in Western Europe; earlier arrangements included the Organization for European Economic Cooperation (since 1960, the Organization for Economic Cooperation and Development), the European Payments Union (since 1958, the European Monetary Agreement), Benelux, and the European Coal and Steel Community set up by the Treaty of Paris in 1952. Yet the EEC, which was established in 1957 by the Treaty of Rome, is by far the most comprehensive plan of economic unification. Countries with full membership in the EEC – Belgium, France, the Federal Republic of Germany, Italy, Luxembourg and the Netherlands – represent a combined population of 184 million and an aggregate income of $300 billion.

The major provisions of the Treaty of Rome include:

(i) Tariffs, quotas and other trade barriers are being gradually eliminated among member countries during a transition period to be completed by mid-1968. The initial 10 per cent reduction occurred in January 1959; by mid-1967, tariffs had been lowered by 85 per cent of their 1957 level.

(ii) A common external tariff (CXT) is being established on imports of products from external sources. The CXT is derived from the arithmetical average of tariffs of the member countries existing at the inception of the Market. However, the mid-1968 CXT will reflect a 20 per cent cut as a result of tariff concessions under the Kennedy Round of the General Agreement on Tariffs and Trade.

(iii) A relatively free movement of labour, services and capital is to exist among member states.

(iv) Domestic economic policies of the six countries are to be harmonized.

(v) Agricultural policies of the member countries are to be coordinated; government assistance will continue to this sector, but will be made uniform throughout the Community.

(vi) A Social Fund has been established to help finance programs for occupational and geographical mobility of workers. The Fund is to ease the readjustment problem for workers who become unemployed due to structural changes which occur as trade is liberalized and industries shift geographically in response to new price-cost relationships.

(vii) Cartels and other restraints of trade are prohibited unless it can be demonstrated that they contribute to an efficiency in the use of resources.

(viii) A number of African states, originally dependent territories of EEC countries, may by mutual agreement remain associated with the EEC. Reciprocal preferential tariff treatment will exist except in instances where the economic advancement of the African states might be accelerated through the use of import restrictions. By mid-1968, all products of the associated states will enter the EEC duty-free.

Full membership in EEC. The Treaty of Rome provides two possible avenues for the inclusion of other countries into the Community, and present members have restated their willingness to consider applications. Article 237 specifies that any European state may apply for membership. This alternative involves full membership and presumes that the applicant countries would accede to most if not all of the provisions of the Treaty of Rome, the Treaty of Paris, and subsequent Community decisions. However, the actual conditions would be determined by negotiation and would be specified in an agreement which must be ratified by each member country. In any event, the unanimity rule applies and applications for membership must be accepted and approved by all existing EEC countries.

Ireland, Denmark and Great Britain applied for membership under Article 237 in 1961. The inclusion of Great Britain was generally considered a prerequisite for Community membership on the part of other members of the European Free Trade Association (EFTA) and of Ireland. Three major factors were at issue in the initial negotiations between Britain and the EEC: the nature of British economic ties to the Commonwealth; the method by which other EFTA participants might be included either as full or as associate members; and an acceptable way of treating the British agricultural sector in the organization. Following several months of deliberation, early hopes for an agreement were destroyed in 1963 when EEC negotiations with Britain were terminated. Ireland's initial application was suspended at that time.

However, the aim of both the British and the Irish governments has generally been that of eventual membership in the EEC. In mid-1967, the British, Irish, Norwegian and Danish governments renewed their formal requests for membership in the EEC. Britain, at the time, appeared willing to make major concessions and with all three political parties in Britain officially endorsing the entry, there seemed to be a greater likelihood of success. Britain also seemed willing to accept the type of agricultural program being implemented by the Community.

In addition, Britain devalued the pound in November of 1967 to improve her balance of payments situation, a condition which was creating concern for some EEC members. It was believed that if Britain were to enter the Common Market, the short-run effect would be to put greater pressure on an already weak balance of payments position. Because of the initial adjustments which her agricultural and industrial sector would have to undertake, it is not unlikely that the British trade position would deteriorate and a serious balance of payments deficit would ensue. Finally, it is argued that the EEC countries, in turn, feel their own progress would be retarded if their policies had to be compromised to accommodate the weak British position.[1] Article 108 of the Treaty of Rome, for example, provides for financial assistance from other EEC members in event one is experiencing balance of payments difficulties.

It became apparent in late 1967 that France was not yet willing to accept Britain as a full member of EEC despite the stated willingness of the British government to make the necessary changes and adaptations. It is generally expected that Britain will not become a member for several years. In the meanwhile the status of Ireland and other applicants remains uncertain.

Inclusion of Great Britain, Norway, Denmark and Ireland in the EEC would have a major impact on the organization. In terms of size alone, the change would be significant; the four countries have an aggregate GNP equivalent to about 40 per cent of the Community's GNP. In addition, the aggregate external trade of the four applicants is somewhat *greater* than that of the Six.

As a full member of the EEC, Ireland would be expected to accept most, if not all, of the provisions of the Treaties of Rome and Paris although there would be a transitional period, determined by negotiation, during which time Irish productive units in agriculture, industry and commerce could make efforts to adapt to the new conditions. Ultimately, all EEC-produced items could be sold duty-free in Ireland and Irish-produced items could be sold duty-free in the huge EEC market. Ireland's external tariff, applicable to non-EEC countries, would be identical to the existing CXT; a national commercial policy would no longer be possible. Ireland would participate in the common agricultural program described later; Irish workers would be relatively free to migrate to and settle permanently in any EEC country, although not with the degree of freedom which has characterized a movement to Britain.

Ireland would also be expected to contribute to the general budget and other funds of the EEC. Ireland's contribution would probably range somewhere between that of Luxembourg, on the one hand, and Belgium or the Netherlands on the other. Of a total $47 million general budget in 1966, the contributions of the three, respectively, were: 0.2 per cent, 8.1 per cent, and 8.2 per cent.

Associate membership in the EEC. The EEC may also conclude an agreement under Article 238 to create an associate status for other countries. Presumably associate status would be appropriate for countries which are unable to accept all of the provisions of the Treaty of Rome, because of political neutrality, or because of an economy unable to compete directly with the EEC industrial structure.

Ireland did at one time, following the breakdown of the British negotiations in 1963, engage in discussions with the EEC in the hope of devising a suitable reciprocal arrangement whereby a certain amount of trade might be conducted on a preferential basis. However, it did not appear at the time that an arrangement could be concluded whereby Ireland could participate in the EEC and yet retain preferential ties with Britain.

Greek association with the EEC. The EEC has concluded agreements of association with two European countries – Greece and Turkey. However, the Greek association is more far-reaching since it provides for full membership on the part of that country after a lengthy (twenty-two year) transition period. The Greek association may have *some* instructive value since a similar type of association could conceivably be suitable for Ireland in the event that Britain is unable to come to terms with the EEC and if Ireland comes to believe that close economic ties with the EEC are of greater value than those with Britain. The EEC has emphasized, however, that the Greek agreement should not be considered as a guide to future associations with other countries.

A treaty was signed in 1962 whereby Greece became attached to the EEC as an associate member under Article 238. The creation of a mutually-acceptable agreement proved to be an arduous task because the Greek economy is largely agricultural and relatively undeveloped in contrast to the relatively industrialized EEC countries. In compliance with the association agreement, the EEC countries have reduced tariffs on imports from Greece to the level corresponding with the Community's internal tariffs (by 1967, an 85 per cent reduction of the 1957 tariff level). Greece, in turn, will have as long as 22 years, if necessary, to abolish completely tariffs on industrial imports. By mid-1967, Greece had reduced tariffs on most industrial imports by 10 per cent and on some items by 30 per cent.

An acceptable arrangement for agriculture has been more difficult to establish, but both sides have made progress in reducing tariffs on food products. It is expected, though, that by the end of the transition period Greek agriculture will be treated on an equal basis with Community agriculture.

Another characteristic of the Community–Greece association is the relatively free movement of workers. The agreement also provided for loans of $125 million to Greece over a five year period. Other special efforts are being made to develop and modernize Greek agriculture and industry and to integrate fully the economy with the EEC by 1984.

There is evidence that despite the concessions and benefits extended by the EEC to help develop and modernize the Greek economy toward the level of the present members, Greece is finding it difficult to make the necessary adjustments. The more progress the EEC makes in implementing the Treaty of Rome, the more difficult it is likely to become for new members to integrate fully into the regional market. Greece had one major advantage in that much of her external trade was already with the EEC countries; in 1961-62, about 33 per cent of her exports were to the Six and about 44 per cent of her imports from the Six. For Ireland, the comparable trade figures with the Six were about 7 per cent and 15 per cent. Political problems in Greece, especially since late 1966, are likely to retard significant progress.

Full or associate status for Ireland. One can only speculate on the relative advantages of full or associate membership for Ireland in the EEC since in either case the terms would be established by negotiation. And in either case, an important factor would be whether or not Britain were to participate. However, it does appear that terms of *full* membership for Ireland could be readily predicted. In short, full membership would in all likelihood require that Ireland accede to all of the provisons of the Treaties of Rome and Paris. However, since Ireland is a relatively small economy and less developed than the EEC countries, she might be given some additional time in which to make adjustments. Irish agriculture would probably benefit most initially as a result of full membership.

If, however, Ireland requires a lengthy period of time to promote structural changes in industry and is unwilling or unable to abolish tariffs on manufactured imports from EEC countries within a short period of time, then an associate status, comparable to that of Greece, might be preferable. The disadvantages of associate status are that Ireland may not have a full voice in the making of Community policy, she may or may not have access to financial resources of the Community which are used to promote occupational and geographical mobility of workers, and finally certain types of long-term financial assistance may not be available to Irish industry. However, there are no predetermined guidelines which would suggest the nature of the possible link between Ireland and the ECC. There have been at least some indications that the Community would follow a flexible approach which could be tailored to fit the requirements of applicant countries.

Commercial ties through trade agreements. Perhaps the minimal commercial tie which Ireland might develop with the EEC is a trade agreement which would specify conditions under which trade in a given number of commodities might be conducted more freely. The EEC has already concluded agreements of this nature with Iran and Israel. In each case, the EEC agreed to provide freer access to a select group of commodity imports, and the two countries, in turn, offered reciprocal concessions to the EEC.

An important feature of the simple trade agreement is that, to comply with the principles of the General Agreement on Tariffs and Trade (GATT), any concessions extended by the countries initiating the agreement must also be extended to the remaining members of GATT. The extension of concessions to all GATT countries complies with most-favoured-nation treatment. This would represent no particular problem if the commodities involved were of interest primarily to Ireland or the EEC countries. If this were not the case, Irish participation in the EEC on the basis of an arrangement other than a simple trade agreement, such as full or associate membership, may be advantageous since tariff reductions would apply only to Ireland and the EEC countries; remaining GATT members would not be included. The reason is that GATT has a special exception allowing members of a free trade area or a common market to remove internal barriers without making the same concessions to remaining GATT members. Thus most-favoured-nation treatment is waived, but only if the external trade barriers employed by the regional groupings are no more restrictive than those previously in force.

The EEC's agricultural program. The EEC's common agricultural program (CAP) is of particular interest to Ireland either in terms of benefits to the economy should Ireland become a member of the organization or in terms of possible adverse effects should she not become a member.[2] The Treaty of Rome stipulates that a common policy be developed to cover the agricultural sectors of the member countries. The CAP is to take the place of the separate national programs which were in existence at the time the Treaty was established. Development of a CAP has proved to be the most difficult of all tasks confronting the EEC members, but by mid-1967 agreement had been reached for commodities covering about 90 per cent of the agricultural output of the six member countries.

The CAP is based on three major provisions: (i) an unrestricted movement of farm products among member countries; (ii) a common commercial policy with respect to agricultural trade with non-member countries; and (iii) joint financing to support internal farm production, to modernize the farm sector, and to subsidize exports to areas outside the EEC. The first objective has been largely achieved as barriers to agricultural trade among member countries have been gradually reduced and will be eliminated by July 1968.

The nature of the common trade policy is of major concern to non-member countries. In 1964, almost 18 per cent of the Community's total imports and 10 per cent of its exports took the form of farm products. The key instrument of commercial policy is the variable levy which is an adjustable import charge designed to raise the price of the imported farm product up to the price level of the Community product. Variable levies have been established for grains, wheat, rice, milk and milk products, pigmeat, eggs and poultry, sugar and olive oil. A fixed common external tariff will apply to beef and veal, and a supplementary levy may also be applied to these products.

As a result of the variable levy, inexpensive commodity imports will not disrupt internal prices; complete protection is also provided to EEC producers since imports can occur only insofar as EEC consumption exceeds Community production. But the key factor determining the protectiveness of the CAP is the extent to which internal support prices (intervention prices) affect Community production in comparison with internal consumption. The variable levy simply prevents cheap imports from disrupting the established program.

The variable levy system is directed primarily toward temperate zone agricultural commodities. On tropical commodities the EEC has pursued a more liberal policy. Duties were abolished on many of these items including tea, maté and tropical hardwoods; they have been reduced significantly on others including cocoa and coffee.

Three types of financial assistance are available in the CAP through the European Agricultural Guidance and Guarantee Fund (EAGGF); domestic price supports, export subsidies, and rationalization of the agricultural sector. The price levels which are supported (the 'intervention' price for most commodities) are uniform throughout the Community and range somewhere between the highest and the lowest initial prices. The establishment of a common price level involves a crucial decision because of its far-reaching impact on Community production and imports, on farm income, and on consumer prices.

During the first years of operations, the greatest share of agricultural financing was directed toward payment of export subsidies. Major Community exports include grains, milk and milk products, fruits and vegetables.

Financing is also available to cover a wide range of projects designed to modernize the agricultural sector including the consolidation of small landholdings, land drainage and conservation as well as the construction of facilities to improve the production, storage, marketing and distribution of commodities.

The details of the manner in which financial resources are to be accumulated have yet to be determined. However, virtually all proceeds accruing from import levies on agricultural commodities will be used for this purpose. The remaining funds may come from import levies on manufactured commodities, from direct contributions by member governments, or from some other source.

Analysis of gains to the economy through agriculture. In general, the Irish agricultural sector, and possibly the entire economy, would benefit, as far as the agricultural program is concerned, if Ireland were to become a member of the EEC. However, participation in the program involves both gains and costs to the Irish economy and is certain to affect the internal distribution of income. The *gain* to the agricultural sector is related to three factors: the availability of higher support prices for many types of commodities; the possibility of a greater volume of exports; and financial assistance for structural reform in agriculture. Such assistance would come from EAGGF. The *cost* to the Irish agricultural sector and the economy at large (as consumers) is the higher price which must be paid for farm products, including both domestic production and imports, and also the financial contribution of Ireland to the EAGGF.

The net benefit of the EAGGF to Ireland can only be estimated.

TABLE XI–1
IRISH PRODUCTION AND EEC PRICES OF SELECT AGRICULTURAL PRODUCTS

Commodity	Irish production, 1967[a]	Nature of EEC price
Cattle Calves	£88.7	Guide price for live cattle, $680.00 per metric ton; for live calves, $915.00. Effective 1 June 1968. Intervention price is 4 to 7% less than guide price.
Milk	71.9	Target price, $10.30 per 100 Kg (3.7% butterfat). Effective 1 June 1968. Support buying for dairy products such that milk can be marketed about $.30 below target price.
Pigs	27.5	Basic price for slaughtered pigs, $735.00 per metric ton. Effective 1 November 1967. Intervention price, when employed, will be between 85 and 90% of basic price.
Sheep	11.8	No common policy established, although one has been requested by some member countries.
Barley	10.9	Intervention price, $87.97 per metric ton. Effective 1 August 1968.
Eggs	9.4	Price depends upon demand and supply, but an import levy provides preference to Community producers.
Wheat (durum)	9.0	Intervention price, $117.50 per Intervention price, $ 117.50 per metric ton. Effective 1 August 1968.
Potatoes	8.1	No common policy established, although one has been requested by some member countries.
Sugarbeet	7.8	Intervention price, $17.00 per metric ton. Effective 1 July 1968.
Poultry	5.7	Price depends upon demand and supply, but an import levy provides preferences to Community producers.

Total	£250.8	
Other	20.5	

Irish production	£271.3	

[a] In millions of pounds.

Sources: European Economic Community. *European Community*. December 1967, p. 6., and April 1968, p. 2; European Community Information Service. *The Common Agricultural Policy* (Community Topics 28), Revised 1967; Central Statistics Office. *Review of 1967 and Outlook for 1968*. Dublin: Stationery Office, 1968, p. 43.

Through 1969, about one-half of the financial resources contributed to the Fund were to be derived from levies placed on agricultural imports. Since Ireland's agricultural imports and import duties from this source are relatively small, this portion of her contribution would not be great. The remainder of the financial requirements was covered by direct contributions from member countries. Ireland's direct contribution would probably approximate that of the existing smaller EEC members which are as follows: Luxembourg, 0.2 per cent of the total; Belgium, 8.1 per cent; and the Netherlands, 8.2 per cent. However, the permanent scheme for financing the agricultural program has yet to be determined, although there is no evidence that it should differ significantly from the present one.

Irish agriculture could expect to benefit substantially from export subsidies and internal support prices covered by the EAGGF. The implications of this particular aspect of the program are suggested in Table XI–1 which shows the major types of commodities produced by Irish agriculture along with the EEC intervention price for such items. The intervention price is that price at which the support agencies are obliged to purchase commodities offered to them. It is somewhat lower than the target price, but might be considered a guaranteed producer pirce. In other words, the Irish farmer would receive, for his *production*, a price no lower than the intervention price. For most agricultural commodities, the intervention price is such that there would likely be an increase in Irish prices, both at the producer and consumer level, as they are aligned with those existing in the Community; a possible exception would be sugar beet in which case the Irish price would be lower.[3]

Insofar as agricultural prices increase in Ireland, domestic consumers would be placed at a disadvantage in that they would pay a higher price for food and other farm products. To the extent that farm produce is consumed domestically, there is no gain to the *entire* economy although there is a redistribution of income from consumers to the farm producer. For domestic consumption the gain to the farmer is a loss to the consumer. The gain to the entire economy would be that accruing from increased foreign exchange earnings as a result of agricultural exports selling at higher prices and also as a result of a greater volume of such exports.

A key consideration, then, is the extent to which the CAP leads to higher export prices and a greater volume of agricultural exports. Major Irish agricultural exports for 1967 are indicated in Table XI–2. It is apparent that the most important potential benefit relates to cattle and beef. In terms of the gain through prices, the

TABLE XI-2

MAJOR AGRICULTURAL EXPORTS, 1967

(in million of pounds)

Cattle	£ 43.6
Beef	42.1
Butter	9.1
Bacon and hams	6.8
Milk and cream	5.3
Cheese	4.8
Horses	4.3
Mutton and lamb	3.8
Wool	3.2
Other agricultural exports	21.2
Total agricultural exports	£ 144.2

Source: Central Statistics Office. *Review of* 1967 *and Outlook for 1968.*
Dublin: 1968, p. 55.

net gain would be equivalent to the export subsidy which would equal the differences between the intervention price and the world market price.

Participation in the EEC would also expand market opportunities for Irish agriculture. The potential in this direction is suggested in Table XI–3 which shows EEC self-sufficiency in farm products of major interest to Ireland. The greatest potential gain for Ireland relates to beef trade; the Six produced only 87 per cent of their own needs for the period 1962/63 to 1963/64. In addition, there is evidence that the demand for beef and also veal is growing more rapidly than production. Expanded opportunities for other items, particularly milk and milk products, are not favourable since the Community is already producing in excess of its own requirements.

Another possible gain to Irish agriculture would be the financial assistance provided to promote structural change and to increase efficiency in agriculture. Under this program, the EAGGF covers 25 per cent of cost of a project with the remainder divided between the respective government and the farmer or group receiving the immediate benefit; there is some evidence that future efforts to aid the farm sector will be directed to a greater extent toward reforming the structure of farming in order to raise productivity. The advantages of this approach, as an alternative to higher support prices, is that it does not lead to higher food prices for consumers, and commodities need not be subsidized so heavily in order to be sold in world markets.

TABLE XI–3
EEC SELF-SUFFICIENCY IN SELECT FARM PRODUCTS[1]

Commodity	Per cent
Beef	87.2
Veal	98.9
Pigmeat	99.8
Milk and milk products	101.9
Sugar	97.1
Poultry	92.4
Eggs	94.2
All cereals (except rice)	86.6

[1]Average, 1962/63 to 1964/65

Source: *European Communities.* Dublin: Stationery Office, 1967, p. 301.

Welfare aspects of regionalism. Although regional trading arrangements provide certain economic advantages to member countries, it is also possible that the consequence is a poorer use of resources and accordingly a reduction in economic welfare. One of the first persons to examine the welfare implications of regional arrangements was Jacob Viner.[4] Viner considers two possibilities:

(i) trade *creation* which might occur when a country becomes a member of a regional union and replaces high-cost domestic production of certain commodities with imports from another member country; and

(ii) trade *diversion* in which a country becoming a member of a union diverts its imports from a low-cost non-union source to a high-cost union source. Since the cost of production is presumed to be the criterion for judging the economic implications, it follows that trade creation implies a gain in economic welfare; trade diversion, a loss.

To illustrate these concepts assume that Britain and Ireland establish a trading arrangement and that when internal barriers are removed Britain starts to buy poultry from Ireland rather than from the U.S. even though the U.S. is the low-cost producer. As a result, the U.S. and Ireland tend to use resources less efficiently and there is a loss in economic welfare. If, on the other hand, Britain was initially producing her own supply of poultry behind high tariff barriers and after establishing a union with Ireland, commences to import poultry from Ireland, the low-cost producer, trade creation takes place. Both Britain and Ireland use resources more efficiently and economic welfare is increased.

Viner's analysis cannot be readily used to determine if the *net* effect of an actual customs union is to raise or to lower economic welfare. For some commodities, trade creation may result; for others, trade diversion. An appropriate weighting to determine the net impact would be virtually impossible. Furthermore, the analysis assumes a perfectly elastic supply of commodities, an assumption which lacks realism.

Nevertheless, Viner's work has contributed to the development of other techniques which have greater usefulness in judging the economic effects of a customs union. Meade and Kreinin have developed a series of propositions or theorems which have the advantage of a greater ease of application.[5] Some of the more interesting theorems are as follows:

(i) the higher the initial duties which are eventually eliminated, the more likely the customs union will raise rather than lower economic welfare;

(ii) the larger the economic area of the union, the more likely a regional arrangement will raise rather than lower economic welfare;

(iii) the greater the difference in average costs of production for identical industries located in different countries in the union prior to the establishment of the union, the more likely an eventual gain in economic welfare.

An examination of the analysis of regionalism seems to suggest that if a customs union is to increase appreciably the economic welfare of participating countries, then some or all member countries must be willing to undertake major structural changes in production and trade patterns to promote a more efficient use of resources. If alterations in production patterns are unnecessary, trade patterns are unlikely to change after unionization, and there is little chance of economic gain. The potential for economic gain from customs unions is based on the assumption of the existence of an inefficient use of resources prior to the establishment of the union. Propositions (i) and (ii) above, for example (which make reference to high initial duties and large differences in production costs for identical industries), imply the existence of inefficiencies in resource use prior to unionization if the arrangement is to provide an opportunity for economic gain. Thus the critical consideration remains that any country expecting to derive significant long-run gains through participation in a customs union may also be expected to undergo major changes in its own internal productive structure. The essential changes relate to buying, producing and marketing procedures. They involve the expansion of some firms and industries, the contraction of others. Export industries are likely to benefit most in the short-run; import competing [in-dustries, especially those which prior to unionization are heavily subsidized or shielded from foreign competition, are likely to bear much of the burden of the adjustment process. In the long-run, resources will shift from these firms to export firms and other firms producing efficiently for the domestic market.

1. For additional details on the sterling problem, see 'Sterling and Europe', *The Irish Banking Review*, March 1967, pp. 14-17.
2. For a comprehensive summary of the Community's agricultural program, see European Community Information Service. *The Common Agricultural Policy* (Community Topics 28). Revised 1967.
3. Commission of the European Communities. *Opinion on the Applications for Membership Received from the United Kingdom, Ireland. Denmark and Norway* (English translation). Brussels; 29 September 1967, pp. 34-39.
4. Jacob Viner. *The Customs Union Issue*. New York: Carnegie Endowment, 1950.
5. James Meade. *The Theory of Customs Unions*. Amsterdam: 1955, and Mordechai Kreinin, 'The Outer-Seven and European Integration,' *American Economic Review*. June 1960, pp. 370-385.

CHAPTER XII

FOREIGN TRADE AND ECONOMIC GROWTH

For any country seeking to accelerate the rate of economic growth, the role of foreign trade requires careful consideration. Among many of today's low-income countries there is a belief that gains from international specialization and exchange have been inadequate; as a result, many low-income countries have pursued policies of industrialization and deliberate import-substitution. Yet there is agreement that most of the present advanced and industrialized countries have benefited from trade which performed the role of a leading sector or engine of growth during their early stages of industrialization.

Exports as a leading sector. The idea of trade as an engine of growth presumes the existence of a dynamic export sector which induces activity in related industries in such a way that economic growth becomes pervasive or promotes development in all other sectors. The dynamic export sector may spring from the discovery of a new commodity or natural resource for overseas sales, changes in tastes of foreign consumers, or technological developments which reduce production costs significantly. In any event, the rate of export growth is sufficient to create profit opportunities in related sectors as a result of what is termed the 'linkage' effect. Basically, the linkage effects reflect the extent to which any given industry interlocks with others within a national economy as a result of inter-industry purchases (backward linkage) and sales (forward linkage).

Some industries are relatively independent; as they experience growth, they do little to contribute to the growth of related industries. However, a more likely situation exists when *either* the backward *or* the forward linkage is low or weak. For an export industry the backward linkages are the most important; if it is to be a leading sector and serve as an engine of growth, the export sector must acquire inputs from other industries – raw materials, power and fuel, transportation, packaging materials, to mention a few. The fact that related industries develop to supply the needs of the export sector gives rise to opportunities for still other industries which need not be directly related to the export sector.

A third inter-industry relation involving what is termed 'lateral' linkages is also possible. The industries developing as a result of the lateral linkages are usually consumer goods producers. As incomes rise in the export sector, workers and owners are able to purchase a greater volume of goods and services thus stimulating expansion in the consumer goods industries.

Exports to finance imports. The literature on Irish planning is not explicit on the role of exports in the programs for economic expansion other than assigning them a key role. It appears, however, that the planners envisage the role of exports not as an engine of growth or a leading sector but rather as a condition for financing the importation of essential items. As implied in the *Second Programme for Economic Expansion*, the role of Irish exports seems to approximate that suggested by W. Arthur Lewis. Lewis proposes that exports are needed not because they directly serve to stimulate investment and consumer income, but rather they are needed to avoid deflationary policies which would otherwise be instituted because of a deterioration in the balance of payments situation. He suggests that, in a country with a narrow resource base, internal investment must be accommodated by additional exports in order to finance the imports of raw materials and foodstuffs stimulated by domestic investment. In the absence of exports, deflationary measures would be required to prevent expanded imports from causing balance of payments difficulties.[1]

The significance of exports to finance imports is suggested in the *Second Programme for Economic Expansion*. It is noted, for example, that 'the sale abroad, through exports, of a substantial portion of GNP is a condition of being able to meet most of the costs of imports required to support investment and consumption needs...' Further, in developing targets for 1970, export projections were made after estimates had been developed for domestic employment, productivity and sectoral growth rates.[2]

The Irish economy, as noted earlier, has a narrow resource base and a high propensity to import. A large share of imports takes the form of producers' goods and materials for further production; imports of such items are essential for economic growth but cannot be produced readily in the internal economy. Had Ireland been able to expand exports in 1965, it would not have been necessary to pursue a contractive domestic policy.

Consideration of exports as a means of obtaining imports rather than as a leading sector may be a realistic approach for a small economy such as Ireland's. The latter approach presumes the existence of strong backward linkages which may not prevail in the small economy. That is, the linkage effect may be transmitted to foreign economies through imports with little impact on the domestic economy. Unless the country is large and possesses a diversity of resources, the import leakage is likely to be high since many kinds of manufacturing industries will not exist locally. The situation with respect to Ireland has been stated in a succinct fashion by Professor C. E. V. Leser:

'Economic growth need not necessarily be led by exports; but without an appropriate expansion in exports, growth can hardly be maintained for any length of time without leading to a balance of payments deficit which, given the level of the capital inflow, is above tolerable limits.'[3]

The difference between the two approaches – exports as a leading sector or to finance imports – may be significant as far as a strategy for growth or criteria for investment are concerned, as well as a difference in terms of what can be expected from exports. In both approaches, however, the export sector plays a key role. Exports as a leading sector implies that growth proceeds throughout the economy almost automatically once export promotion has been undertaken in the appropriate industries. Planners can concentrate on stimulating activity in those export sectors with strong backward linkages and anticipate that the profit and investment opportunities created in related sectors will lead to pervasive growth.

The other approach – exports to finance imports – implies that growth may not be automatically transmitted throughout the economy because of a high import leakage. Exports are considered a necessary but not a sufficient condition of growth. Internal development must be promoted along with the export sector but the balance of payments position becomes the major determinant of the level of domestic activity. Consumer spending for non-essentials, both domestic and imported, may need to be held in check, and export proceeds may have to be allocated carefully among the variety of competing needs.

Furthermore, a recognition that the export sector is not a leading sector implies that a 'rounded' structure of development – one encompassing the full range of consumer and producer goods industries – may not be economically feasible for the small economy. Instead, the import sector must fill the gaps in the productive structure where production is technologically or economically impossible. Industries affected to the greatest extent by the smallness of a country have been identified by Chenery as those producing machinery, transportation equipment and intermediate commodities. Those least affected include services, agriculture and many types of consumer goods.[4] Accordingly, import substitution, insofar as it is undertaken in a conscious, deliberate fashion, would need to be conducted on a selective basis to avoid the encouragement of firms which could not continue operations in the face of foreign competition.

Foreign exchange impact. One method of evaluating the feasibility of the emphasis on industrial exports to provide foreign exchange for imports is to analyze the balance of payments impact of such a program. The potential growth opportunities afforded by various types of exports varies from commodity to commodity but depends upon the magnitude of exchange earnings which can be acquired from foreign sales. The volume of exchange earnings, in turn, is a function both of supply conditions (in the domestic economy) and of demand conditions (in the foreign market).

On the demand side, the major consideration is the extent to which changes in foreign income affect the composition of aggregate spending. Some products are income *elastic*; they absorb a relatively larger share of aggregate spending as incomes rise (reflecting Engel's Law). Such items enjoy a market which grows more rapidly than world income and accordingly provide a great potential for earning foreign exchange for producing nations.

The nature of supply conditions in the exporting country is an equally important determinant of the growth potential of alternative commodities. The most favorable type of commodity export is one which is produced domestically under conditions of decreasing or constant unit costs. The least favorable type of export is one the output of which can be expanded only by incurring rapidly increasing costs; the supply of a commodity of this type is *inelastic* with respect to price.

Thus the potential of a given commodity export to contribute to a favorable balance of payments situation is dependent upon the combined influences of the conditions of foreign demand for, and domestic supply of, that commodity. In more technical but precise terms, the more elastic is foreign demand for a given commodity, the greater the long-run opportunity to earn foreign exchange; the opportunity is even more favorable when domestic supply is elastic with respect to price.[5]

The planned expansion in Irish exports appears to be compatible with the types of demand and supply elasticities required for a maximum expansion in foreign exchange earnings. In 1963, agricultural exports represented about 59 per cent of total exports; this share is projected to decline to 47 per cent by 1970. Industrial exports, which in 1963 amounted to 33 per cent would increase to 44 per cent by 1970. Within the industrial category, the major relative increases in recent years have been with respect to textiles, cutlery, hardware, implements and machinery, fertilizers and chemicals.

155

Empirical evidence suggests that the relevant demand and supply elasticities for these items appear to support the shift in export emphasis as a strategy for expanding foreign exchange earnings. There is evidence that the income elasticity of demand is lower for agricultural products than for manufactured items. Although the elasticity of demand for meat and meat products is higher than that of many other food products, it is lower than that for most manufactured and finished items.

Generalizations concerning the elasticity of supply cannot be made as readily. According to some studies, however, the coefficient of price elasticity of supply is highest for finished and semi-finished manufactures; lowest, for primary commodites.[6]

Thus Ireland's new export emphasis would appear to be on items for which foreign demand is income elastic; the domestic supply, price elastic. Insofar as the programme is successful, it should contribute to a greater volume of exchange earnings with which to finance imports.

Relation of exports and economic growth. While the target increase in GNP during the period 1960 through 1970 is 50 per cent, the estimated required growth in exports is 100 per cent. In other words, a 1 per cent growth in GNP is associated with a 2 per cent increase in the value of exports. It is interesting to compare this relationship with the results of an independent empirical study which relates export growth to growth in domestic activity. According to this study, which covers a group of 50 countries for the years 1953-1963, for every 2.5 per cent increase in exports, *per capita* real GNP showed an increase of 1 per cent; furthermore, a high degree of statistical reliability was present.[7] Ireland's per capita target GNP is not specified in the *Second Programme for Economic Expansion*. If, however, the size of the population does expand somewhat between 1960 and 1970, the 2.5 to 1 ratio of the change in exports to the change in per capita income would closely correspond with a comparable ratio for Ireland.

Trade and unemployment. Although the linkage coefficients are high for industrial exports which the Irish government is promoting, the corresponding structural changes and internal growth may be disappointing if a large share of the inputs is purchased from abroad (that is, if the import content of exports is high). Thus an integral part of the emphasis on external sales of manufactured items is the extensive use of indigenous labour, raw materials and capital.

Another model by which exports promote economic growth is somewhat explicit in Irish planning. This model assumes unemployed or underemployed resources initially. An expanding, modern export sector absorbs resources from areas where they are unemployed or their productivity is low. Thus the volume of exports can be increased with no reduction in output of other sectors. Unless the commodity terms of trade deteriorate, the level of imports can increase.[8]

Ireland is an economy with a high rate of unemployment of workers and a large number are being released annually from the agricultural sector. The target growth rate of GNP is projected to involve a 1.1 per cent increase in employment along with a 3.2 per cent increase in productivity.[9] Much of the increased employment would take place in the industrial sector which, in turn, is dependent upon industrial exports increasing by 150 per cent during the period 1960-1970.

Trade and the capacity to transform. However, as far as exports promoting internal growth, the critical consideration is not simply the extent to which export sectors use existing internal resources, but also the extent to which activity in the export sectors serves to *alter and restructure* existing resources and the surrounding environment to create conditions conducive to rapid growth. Baldwin, for example, suggests instances in which a set of export industries, frequently exporting agricultural materials, adapted to the prevailing labour endowment and did little to provide an impetus for eliminating the backwardness of the labour force. But Baldwin argues that a completely different type of export activity – one requiring skilled labour, entrepreneurial ability and capital – may do equally little to promote pervasive development because it may have an impact on such a small part of the economy with much of the specialized inputs imported from abroad.[10]

Thus it may be that the export sectors which promote development are those which not only utilize but also develop an indigenous supply of skilled workers, which stimulate the creation of a vigorous native entrepreneurship, and which foster attitudes of thrift and optimism that are essential for growth. There is some evidence, for example, that an improvement in the mobility and adaptibility of the Irish labour force, and a general change in attitudes would create conditions which are more favourable to economic expansion.[11]

An economy's potential for development and growth thus rests largely on its capacity to transform and adapt itself to new opportunities which are created both in the foreign markets and in the domestic economy. An open economy, highly dependent upon external markets, is in even greater need of a productive structure which is flexible, adaptable and capable of adjusting to changing external market conditions.

1. W. Arthur Lewis. 'International Competition in Manufactures,' *American Economic Review*. XLVII, 1957, pp. 578-587.
2. *Second Programme for Economic Expansion*. Dublin: Stationery Office, 1963. Part I, pp. 46-47. Part II, pp. 286-297, 309-327.
3. C. E. V. Leser. *A Study of Imports*. Dublin: The Economic and Social Research Institute, April 1967, p. 20.
4. H. B. Chenery, 'Patterns of Industrial Growth,' *American Economic Review*. September 1960, pp. 624-654.
5. See, for example, Charles P. Kindleberger. *Economic Development* (Second edition). New York: McGraw-Hill, 1965, pp. 295-321.
6. As an illustration, Stern assumes the following elasticities of supply: crude materials, foodstuffs, and animals, .O; semi-manufactures, .20; non-durable finished manufactures, .25; and durable finished manufactures, .50. The assumed estimates were for the United States and may, of course, be different for other countries. See Robert M. Stern. 'The U.S. Tariff and the Efficiency of the U.S. Economy,' *American Economic Review*. May 1964, pp. 459-470.
7. Robert F. Emery. 'The Relation of Exports and Economic Growth,' *Kyklos*. 1967, pp. 470-484.
8. This model is described by Charles P. Kindleberger. 'Foreign Trade and Economic Growth: Lessons from Britain and France, 1850 to 1913,' *Economic History Review*. Vol. XIV, December 1961, pp. 289-305.
9. *Second Programme for Economic Expansion, A Digest*. Dublin: Stationery Office, 1964, p. 24.
10. Robert E. Baldwin. *Economic Development and Export Growth*. Berkeley: University of California Press, 1966, pp. 58-73.
11. See, for example, National Industrial Economic Council. *Report on Full Employment*. Dublin: Stationery Office, 1967, p. 57-59.

BIBLIOGRAPHY
A. Works on Ireland

Commission of the European Communities. *Opinion on the Applications for Membership Received from the United Kingdom, Ireland, Denmark and Norway* (English translation). Brussels: September 1967.

Crotty, Raymond D. *Irish Agricultural Production*. Cork, Ireland: Cork University Press, 1967.

Department of Finance. *Economic Development*. Dublin: Stationery Office, 1958.

Donaldson, Loraine. *Development Planning in Ireland*. New York: Frederick A. Praeger, 1965.

Duncan, G. A. 'The Small State and International Equilibrium,' *Economia Internazionale*, 3 (November 1950), pp. 933-951.

Hein, John. *Institutional Aspects of Commercial and Central Banking in Ireland*. Dublin: Economic and Social Research Institute, January 1967.

Hogan, G. P. S. 'The Administration of Exchange Control in Ireland,' *Public Administration in Ireland* (Frederick King, ed.), III, Dublin: The Richview Press, 1954, pp. 109-128.

Irish Export Board. *Annual Report*. Dublin: Published annually.

Johnston, Joseph. *Why Ireland Needs the Common Market*. Cork, Ireland: The Mercier Press, Ltd., 1962.

Kaim-Caudle, P. R. *Social Security in Ireland and Western Europe*. Dublin: Economic and Social Research Institute, June 1964.

Leser, C. E. V. *A Study of Imports*. Dublin: Economic and Social Research Institute, April 1967.

–, *Imports and Economic Growth in Ireland*, 1947-61. Dublin: Economic and Social Research Institute, June 1963.

–, 'Recent Demographic Developments in Ireland,' *Journal of the Statistical and Social Inquiry of Ireland*, XXI, Part III, pp. 179-201.

National Industrial Economic Council. *Report on Full Employment*. Dublin: Stationery Office, 1967.

Nevin, Edward. *Textbook of Economic Analysis* (Irish edition). London: Macmillan & Co., Ltd., 1963.

–, *The Irish Tariff and the E.E.C.: A Factual Survey*. Dublin: Economic and Social Research Institute, January 1962.

O'Mahony, David. *Economic Aspects of Industrial Relations*. Dublin: Economic and Social Research Institute, February 1965.

–, *The Irish Economy* (Second edition). Cork, Ireland: The Cork University Press, 1967.

Organization for Economic Cooperation and Development. 'Ireland,' *Economic Survey*, Paris. Published annually.

Perry, Patrick. 'Development Programs in Ireland,' *International Monetary Fund Staff Papers* (March 1965), pp. 119-162.

Riordan, E. J. *Modern Irish Trade and Industry*. London: Methuen & Co., Ltd., 1920.

B. General Works

Avramovic, Dragoslav, *et al. Economic Growth and External Debt*. Baltimore, Md.: Johns Hopkins Press, 1964.

Ball, R. J. and Pamela Drake. 'Export Growth and the Balance of Payments,' *The Manchester School*, XXX (May 1962), pp. 105-120.

Demas, William G. *The Economics of Development in Small Countries*. Montreal, Canada: McGill University Press, 1965.

Deutsch, Karl W., Chester I. Bliss, and Alexander Eckstein. 'Population, Sovereignty, and the Share of Foreign Trade,' *Economic Development and Cultural Change*. July 1962, pp. 353-366.

Emery, Robert F. 'The Relation of Exports and Economic Growth,' *Kyklos*, XX, 1967, pp. 470-484.

Fleming, J. Marcus. 'Toward Assessing the Need for International Reserves,' *Essays in International Finance*. Princeton, N.J.: Princeton University Press, 1967.

Friedlander, Stanley L. *Labor Migration and Economic Growth*. Cambridge, Mass.: The Massachusetts Institute of Technology Press, 1965.

Gold, Bela. 'Industrial Growth Patterns: Theory and Empirical Results,' *Journal of Industrial Economics* (November 1964), pp. 53-73.

Haring, Joseph E. 'Export Industrialism and Economic Growth: A Dynamic Model,' *Western Economic Journal* (Spring 1963), pp. 114-126.

Ingram, James C. *Regional Payments Mechanisms* (The Case of Puerto Rico). Chapel Hill, N.C.: University of North Carolina, 1962.

Isard, Walter, *et al. Methods of Regional Analysis*. New York: Technology Press and John Wiley, 1960.

Kindleberger, Charles P. *Foreign Trade and the National Economy*. New Haven, Conn.: Yale University Press, 1962.

–, *International Economics*. Homewood, Ill.: Richard D. Irwin, Inc., 1963.

Lefeber, Louis. *Location and Regional Planning*. Athens: Center of Planning and Economic Research, 1966.

Lewis, W. Arthur. 'Economic Development With Unlimited Supplies of Labour,' *The Manchester School* (May 1954), pp. 131-191.

Lindberg, Leon N. *The Political Dynamics of European Economic Integration*. Stanford, Calif.: Stanford University Press, 1963.

Machlup, Fritz. 'The Need for Monetary Reserves,' *Banca Nazionale del Lavora Quarterly Review*, 77 (September 1966), pp. 175-222.

Maizels, Alfred. *Industrial Growth and World Trade*. Cambridge: Cambridge University Press, 1963.

Meier, Gerald. *International Trade and Development*. New York: Harper & Row, 1963.

Ohlin, Bertil. *Interregional and International Trade*. Cambridge, Mass.: Harvard University Press, 1933.

Paglin, Morton. ''Surplus' Agricultural Labor and Development: Facts and Theories,' *American Economic Review* (September 1965), pp. 815-834.

Robinson, Austin (ed.). *The Economic Consequences of the Size of Nations*. International Economic Association. London: Macmillan & Co., Ltd., 1963.

Rothschild, K. W. 'The Small Nation and World Trade', *Economic Journal*, 54 (April 1944), pp. 26-34.

Thomas, Brinley. *Migration and Economic Growth*. Cambridge: Cambridge University Press, 1954.

Tiebout, Charles M. 'Exports and Regional Economic Growth,' *Journal of Political Economy* (April 1956), pp. 160-169.

Wallich, Henry C. *Monetary Problems of an Export Economy*. Cambridge, Mass.: Harvard University Press, 1950.

Waterson, Albert. *Development Planning – Lessons of Experience*. Baltimore, Md.: The Johns Hopkins Press, 1965.

Watkins, Melville H. 'A Staple Theory of Economic Growth,' *Canadian Journal of Economics and Political Science*, XXIX (May 1963), pp. 141-158.

Whitman, Marina von Neumann. 'International and Interregional Payments Adjustments: A Synthetic View,' *Princeton Studies in International Finance*. Princeton, N.J.: Princeton University Press, 1967.